POWERFUL

PARAGRAPHS

WITHDRAWN

ALSO BY BRUCE ROSS-LARSON

Edit Yourself
Riveting Reports
Stunning Sentences

THE   EFFECTIVE   WRITING   SERIES

POWERFUL

PARAGRAPHS

BRUCE ROSS-LARSON

W. W. NORTON & COMPANY • NEW YORK • LONDON

The text of this book is composed in Electra
with the display set in Futura
Composition by RRDonnelley & Sons, Allentown Digital Services Division
Manufacturing by the Haddon Craftsmen, Inc.
Book design by JAM Design

Library of Congress Cataloging-in-Publication Data

Ross-Larson, Bruce Clifford, 1942–
   Powerful paragraphs / Bruce Ross-Larson.
      p.   cm. — (The effective writing series)
   ISBN 0-393-31794-3 (pbk.)
   1. English language — Paragraphs — Problems, exercises, etc. 2. English
language — Rhetoric — Problems, exercises, etc. 3. Report writing — Problems,
exercises, etc. I. Title. II. Series: Ross-Larson, Bruce Clifford, 1942– Effective
writing series.
PE1439.R67   1999
808'.042 — dc21   98-35265
                                                        CIP

W. W. Norton & Company, Inc., 500 Fifth Avenue, New York, N.Y. 10110
www.wwnorton.com

W. W. Norton & Company Ltd., 10 Coptic Street, London WC1A 1PU

1 2 3 4 5 6 7 8 9 0

For Veruschka
and all my colleagues at the
American Writing Institute

CONTENTS

AUTHOR'S NOTE

THE techniques presented here, refined in the workshops I've conducted over the past fifteen years, are intended to help you write paragraphs that are unified, coherent, and well developed. The questions about identifying a paragraph's topic and point— and about determining whether each of a paragraph's sentences bears on that point—should help you spot problems and quickly solve them. The patterns of paragraph development should allow you to inject your writing with variety and interest. And the suggested transitions between paragraphs should enable you to extend the coherence of your argument, making it easier for your readers to follow. If you run across exemplars of the paragraph models identified here—or find interesting variants, indeed new species—please send them to me at bruce@cdinet.com or browse into (www.cdinet.com/AmericanWritingInstitute). I'll try to plug them into the next edition.

I'd like to acknowledge the contributions of my colleagues at the American Writing Institute: Amy Cracknell, Andrea Brunholzl, Jessica Moore, Erika Schelble, Alison Smith, Kelli Ashley, and the interns Brendan McCarthy, Adam Calderon, Jessica Henig, and Ana Dahlman. I'd also like to acknowledge those of my editorial colleagues at Communications Development who reviewed the manuscript throughout its many stages: Meta de Coquereaumont, Alison Strong, Paul Holtz, Daphne Levitas, and Heidi Gifford. And I'd like to thank Xan Smiley and *The Economist* for the permission to reproduce the piece attached at the back and the many writers credited with the individual paragraphs I've used as examples.

BRUCE ROSS-LARSON
Washington, D.C.

POWERFUL

PARAGRAPHS

AN APPROACH TO PARAGRAPHS

MANY writers think of paragraphs as a collection of sentences framed by an indent and a carriage return, running perhaps ten or twelve lines. Few have the language to describe what's good—or bad—about a paragraph. This book shows you what it means for a paragraph to be unified, coherent, and well developed. The idea here is to give you a way of looking at paragraphs that will change the way you write.

A paragraph is unified if each sentence is clearly related to the point, coherent if you make it obvious to your reader how each sentence is linked to the point. You can make the link more obvious by repeating key words and phrases. You can also use transitional words and phrases to enumerate and coordinate a paragraph's sentences. And you can change the structure of your sentences to reveal parallel or subordinate ideas. These techniques do more than make your paragraphs coherent—they also give them pace.

A paragraph is well developed if its sentences unfold in a way that makes your argument perfectly clear to the reader. One of the best ways to do this is to express the point of the paragraph as a general statement in the first sentence and then to support it with details and examples in subsequent sentences. Used for perhaps half to two-thirds of all paragraphs in expository writing, this model is among the most common. Some of the other ways are to conclude with the point, to phrase the point as a question and answer, and to undermine an argument to make the opposite point. Still other ways include making a subtle (or not so subtle) comment at the end of a straightforward series of details. Deciding how you develop a paragraph generally depends on the details, examples, and comments you have to support your point.

BUILDING PARAGRAPHS FROM A PLAN

Strong paragraphs will emerge more easily if you have done some planning. (*Riveting Reports*, also in this series, is a good place to start.) A paragraph-by-paragraph plan helps you organize your material by going beyond an outline to identify the topic of each paragraph in an entire piece. You then write the topic of each paragraph at the top of a sheet of paper (or page screen, if you're online) and try to make a strong point about each topic. Finally you assemble your raw material — details, comments, examples — under those points. With your material thus organized, and your head significantly clearer, you're ready to write unified, coherent, well-developed paragraphs.

GETTING OFF TO A GOOD START

Opening paragraphs have tremendous effect on how — and whether — your piece will be read. The most common opening is the throat-clearing paragraph that blandly announces how the piece will unfold. What you want instead is to grab your readers' attention, rivet them to your message, and propel them through your argument. Here are a few ways to do just that.

Put your main message up front. Tell your readers exactly what you intend to get across to them by setting out your main and any supporting messages up front, where they can't be missed.

In no society today do women enjoy the same opportunities as men. This unequal status leaves considerable disparities between how much women contribute to human development and how little they share in its benefits.

Start with a gripping fact. Present a compelling (or even shocking) fact or statistic that you suspect your readers will find interesting.

Every twenty minutes or so, someone somewhere is killed or injured by a landmine. According to the United Nations more than 110m buried mines are left over from the 20th century's numerous wars—most of them in poor countries such as Afghanistan, Angola and Cambodia which can ill afford the cost of removing them.

Ask questions. Ask questions to draw your readers in as participants, enticing them to read on and find out the answers.

Swamped by voicemail and email? Prepare yourself for the next wave of digital communications deluge: instant messaging.

Set the scene. Descriptive details can pull readers in by helping them to visualize the scene you're setting.

Out here in Big Sky Country, high on a ridge in the Absaroka Range, a golden eagle soars, pushed upward by a stream of warm air. From its perch in a golden-leafed aspen, a Steller's jay the color of indigo shrieks at the interlopers 20 feet below.

A Clark's nutcracker drills into a pine cone, the only sound except the distant rumble from the Yellowstone River.

Surprise your readers. Humor can put your readers at ease, a tactic especially useful before launching into a controversial topic.

The bagpipe's appeal is difficult to explain. Playing it can be a lonely calling. At a party, nobody asks you to sit down and bang out a song. You wear a skirt. There are the jokes.

Present a brief history. Starting with a historical anecdote adds the interest of analogy—and boosts your credibility.

Even the early stages of the Industrial Revolution quickly made England the wealthiest society that had ever existed, but it took a long time for the wealth to be reflected in the earnings of ordinary workers. Economic historians still argue about whether real wages rose or fell between 1790 and 1830, but the very fact that there is an argument shows that the laboring classes did not really share in the nation's new prosperity.

It's happening again. As with early 19th century England, late 20th century America is a society being transformed by radical new technologies that have failed to produce a dramatic improvement in the lives of ordinary working families—indeed, these are the technologies whose introductions have been associated with stagnant or declining wages for many. The Industrial Revolution was not based on silicon and information; but in a deep sense the story is probably much the same.

Address your readers. Use the imperative to involve your readers personally.

Imagine it is late 1986 and you are managing a consumer electronics factory in Japan. Your business is in trouble. The deal struck at the Plaza Hotel the year before has doubled the value of the yen—the currency your manufacturing costs are based in—against the dollar, the currency of your biggest export market. Your workers are expensive and it is hard to find anyone to do jobs that involve the three ks—*kitamai, kiken, kitsui* (dirty, dangerous, or tough). The currencies of your most aggressive competitors, the Taiwanese and Koreans, have risen only slightly against the dollar and they are snatching market share away from you. What do you do?

Open with a quotation. Using someone else's well-put words can handily set the tone for what follows.

"Unsex me!" cried Lady Macbeth in a plea to the spirits that should probably be inscribed in the Pentagon somewhere.

"Character," says Aristotle, *"gives us qualities, but it is in actions—what we do—that we are happy or the reverse."* We have already decided that Aristotle is wrong and now we must face the consequences of disagreeing with him.

SUMMING UP

Powerful closing paragraphs convey the essence of an argument's main points without restating all of its detail. The strongest closing paragraphs put the main points in a broader perspective and provoke further thought.

Restate the essence of your main message. The most common kind of closing paragraph restates the conclusions of a report. Try to restate only the essence of your main messages, using new language or a new image.

There is a curve of time that separates Heman Sweatt and Cheryl Hopwood. It has been a long while since that spring afternoon in 1950 when, as a first-year Yale law student, I heard the promise of freedom in the voice of Thurgood Marshall. Since then, I have observed commendable progress, lately some tragic retrogression, and now I see even more clearly that, in the long, bloody history of the race relations in America, there is no more time for foolishness.

This example also pulls in the title of the report ("Achieving Analytical Wisdom"), linking the last line of the closing paragraph to the very beginning of the report. Readers will feel as though they have come full circle and will have a sense of completion.

Use a closing quotation. Sometimes someone else has already summed up the message of your piece quite well. If so, use it.

In the meantime, expatriates like Bowles and McPhillips cling stubbornly to their adopted city. "It still has this attraction, this inexplicable ability to pull at your heart and soul," McPhillips says. "There's the light, the air, the wind blowing through the strait, the interplay between Europe and Morocco that will never change. Tangier is indestructible."

This quotation offers proof of the writer's concluding idea:

Will the wily Mr. Castro change with the times? He seems to be incapable of it—incapable of abandoning his ideology even for the sake of increasing his chances of maintaining power. Fidel himself puts it this way. "It is the world that is changing. Cuba will not change . . . even death will not defeat us."

Pose a question. One question, or a series of questions, will suggest ways to branch from your argument or its possible trajectories. Or, as in this example, it can be used as a comment to linger in people's minds.

> The real differences between the mergers of the 1980s and previous waves do not lie either in the hostility of the bids or the nature of the financing. They lie in why the restructuring took place and in the forms of ownership and capital structure that were assumed to be superior to the old. As an Irish prime minister once said after listening to a long debate between his cabinet colleagues: "I understand how it works in practice. But how does it work in theory?"

Propose a challenge or future direction. Put your purpose into words by giving readers something concrete to do after reading your report.

> But the aim should be for the UN, through the Security Council, to decide where a UN-sponsored force should be deployed and have the capacity to man it, not to subcontract the job and the decision-making to individual members. Turning the UN into cheerleader, or belated picker-up of superpowers' problems, is not the way to improve peacekeeping. The UN's authority needs to be strengthened, not sidestepped.

At the end of this book, you'll find another sampling of paragraph models that can give your writing more variety and pace. Many of the techniques embodied in those models can bridge two paragraphs or develop an argument across a series of paragraphs. In between, you will learn how to identify the points of your paragraphs, how to present those points strongly, and how to support your points in clear, compelling ways to create powerful paragraphs.

1

UNIFY YOUR PARAGRAPHS AROUND STRONG POINTS

POINTLESS. That is one of the biggest problems a writer has with paragraphs: failing to tell readers the point of what they're reading. Close behind is having a point with no support: a succession of loose, even unrelated, sentences.

The solution to the first problem is simply to add a strong point—and to make it obvious, usually by leading with it. The solution to the second problem is to make sure that every sentence in a paragraph bears on the point—and then to clarify the supporting sentences by using the traditional rhetorical devices of repeating a key term, counting the elements, signaling what's to come, and changing the structure of sentences. These devices also make your paragraphs easier to read—and more likely to stay in your reader's mind.

BE CLEAR ABOUT YOUR SUBJECT

Writers rarely take the time to figure out the subject of a paragraph before they write one. But only by knowing the subject can you make a strong point about it. And only with a strong point can you assess whether all of a paragraph's sentences are related to it.

In the following paragraphs the subject is **boldfaced** and the point *italicized*. (In the first two sections of this book I have *italicized* what I surmise to be the point of many of the paragraphs.)

> **Manchuria** *openly displays its attachment to a bygone age.* In the port of Dalian, in Liaoning province, there is a Stalin Street; and in Shenyang, the province's capital, stands one of the few remaining public statues of Mao. In Harbin, the capital of Heilongjiang, a party official says that Mao's poems, set to music, are as suitable for karaoke sessions as "Love Story"; to prove it, he sings one.

> **Jeff Pulver** *is well and truly wired.* He is an Internet entrepreneur, with his fingers in many pipes, particularly the "fat pipe" that snakes into his home in Great Neck, New York. The fat pipe is a wire that can carry 1.5 bits of data a second. In lots of companies a pipe that fat is shared by hundreds of employees. Mr. Pulver has one all to himself. He thinks of it as rather expensive insurance against his Internet's principal curse: delay.

MAKE A STRONG POINT

Powerful paragraphs need more than obvious subjects—they need strong points. Usually stated explicitly at the start, sometimes implied, the point is a statement of opinion or fact, which you then support with the other sentences in your paragraph.

> *The growth of America's capital in recent years has indeed been remarkable.* The District of Columbia bar had fewer

than 1,000 members in 1950, now it has 61,000. The number of journalists in Washington soared from 1,500 to 12,000 over the same period. The staff of Congress has roughly doubled since 1979. On one estimate, 91,000 lobbyists of one sort or another grace the Washington area with their presence.

By almost any measure, *Chile in 1995 has an economy that it is difficult to find fault with.* Inflation is in single digits and declining. Foreign reserves at $14.8 billion are high and rising. The government consistently runs a healthy budget surplus. Exports grew by more than 25% last year. Foreign investment was $4.7 billion (9.1% of GDF). The unemployment rate, less than 6%, is one of the lowest in Latin America.

"Ulysses" has a long history of translation. It was greeted as a great work of literary modernism when it appeared in its highly original English in 1922. But it was available in German and French before it was legally for sale in Britain or the United States. Even the Latvians have their own version; the Japanese have four. Chinese translators never got around to it. After the Communist victory in 1949, such a work would have been dangerous.

BE SURE EVERY SENTENCE BEARS
ON THE POINT

After you've written a paragraph, check to be sure each sentence supports the point. Too often, sentences are loosely related to the subject of the paragraph but not tied to the point.

In the following examples, the supporting sentences have been rated *yes* (Y) if clearly related, *no* (N) if unrelated, and *questionable* (?) if their relationship to the point is dubious.

Game theory, fathered 50 years ago by the great mathematician John von Neumann, *has become an important tool for economists and businesses.* Businesses apply it in sharpening their marketplace skills, drawing on available information, as a poker player does, to plot their next moves and guess the reaction of competitors. [Y] Economists use it in a broader sense to forecast interactions of all kinds. [Y] Strategists at Rand Corp. and elsewhere have applied it to anticipate the diplomatic and military moves of governments. [Y]

In the paragraph above, all the sentences clearly relate to the point. The pronoun *it* anchors *game theory* in each of the supporting sentences, which show how game theory has become an important tool.

Business is very bad at Porsche. Sales of the speedy luxury cars on which the company built its reputation have fallen by more than half in the space of just two years. [Y] The cars are known for their sporty design and superior performance. [N] The work force has been cut by 25 percent. [Y] Inside the plant workers are nervous and insecure. [?]

Sometimes unrelated sentences stick out grotesquely; others require scrutiny to ferret them out. In the preceding paragraph, the third sentence—on *sporty design*—sends the reader off course and diffuses the point. It should be cut. The fifth sentence may be true, but it would be more effective pulled into the fourth: ". . . *by 25 percent, leaving workers inside the plant nervous and insecure.*"

The life blood of a Chinese company is guanxi—*connections.* Penetrating layers of *guanxi* is like peeling an onion: first come connections between people with ancestors from the same province in China; then people from the same clan or village;

finally, the family. [Y] It does not matter much whether a Chinese businessman is in Hong Kong or New York, he will always operate through *guanxi*. [Y] But these networks do not enforce conformity. [?] Chinese tend to be far less concerned with consensus than the Japanese. [N] As long as they honor their word and look after their own, they can do whatever they want. [N]

The second and third sentences clearly support the point—that *connections* are *the life blood of a Chinese company*. The fourth might be sliding into another point—and could open another paragraph. The fifth and sixth sentences deal with this second, albeit related point and undermine the paragraph's coherence.

REPEAT A KEY TERM

Once you've rid a paragraph of extraneous material, try repeating a key word or phrase to bind the sentences even more. Many writers have an aversion to repetition, something they generally acquire in the seventh grade. But using different terms for the same idea simply to avoid repetition will confuse your reader.

In this example, repeating the term *Mother's Day* ties the four sentences together.

> *On Mother's Day this year MCI*, America's second-largest long-distance telephone company, *offered many of its domestic customers free calls.* Struck by an annual outbreak of filial sentiment, Americans make more long-distance calls on *Mother's Day* than on any other day of the year. Americans also have almost a quarter of the world's telephone lines, so *Mother's*

Day traffic in the United States is probably the heaviest anywhere in the world. Yet MCI felt it could offer a free service on *Mother's Day* without overloading its network.

The next version, by contrast, is loose — because it avoids repetition. The use of *that day* is fine in the second sentence, tying it to the first. But the third has no tie to *Mother's Day*, weakening the attempted link of *this holiday* in the fourth.

On Mother's Day this year MCI, America's second-largest long-distance telephone company, *offered many of its domestic customers free calls.* Struck by an annual outbreak of filial sentiment, Americans make more long-distance calls on that day than on any other day of the year. Americans also have almost a quarter of the world's telephone lines, so traffic in the United States is probably the heaviest anywhere in the world. Yet MCI felt it could offer a free service on this holiday without overloading its network.

Repeating more than one word can create a resounding echo:

In Europe's first integration at the hands of bureaucratic Roman imperialists these quickening virtues had been stifled and therein lay the seeds of the empire's dissolution. Therein too lay the kernel of an oblique message for Gibbon's contemporaries. And our contemporaries too?

The repetition of *therein* and *lay* ties the second sentence to the first, and the repetition of *too* and *contemporaries* ties the third to the second.

For 34 years he lived in the uneasy crucible of Congress, first tasting the frustrations of powerlessness and then exercising the prerogatives of power. He took his lessons through the haze of Camel cigarettes and over the bourbon and branch water that flowed in Sam Rayburn's secret hideaway. He took others from another master of leadership, Lyndon B. Johnson. Later, he dispensed lessons of his own, and sometimes they were lessons in brutal partisanship; his Republican rivals learned them not wisely but too well.

In the paragraph above, the subject of each sentence, *he*, ties all four sentences together. The repetition of *took* ties the third sentence to the second, and that of *lessons* ties the fourth.

REPEAT A SENTENCE STRUCTURE—FOR SENTENCES DOING THE SAME WORK

If sentences are doing similar work, they're easier to understand if they're similar in structure. As with repeating a key word or term, repeating a structure can strengthen the links among your supporting sentences and between those sentences and your point.

Here are some supportive sentences that open differently:

History has a capricious memory, and it's anyone's guess how it will remember James C. Wright Jr. of Texas. It may remember him grandly, because he was the House Speaker who most aggressively muscled his way into foreign policy. If he is remembered more simply, it will be as one of the forgotten figures who served between two white-haired partisans, Thomas P. O'Neill Jr. of Massachusetts and Newt Gingrich of Georgia. Or he may be poignantly remembered as the forlorn man who was toppled from the giddiest heights of American politics . . . over a book.

Not unreadable, but not nearly as unified or memorable as:

*History has a capricious memory, and it's anyone's guess how it
will remember James C. Wright Jr. of Texas.* Perhaps grandly, as
the House Speaker who most aggressively muscled his way
into foreign policy. Perhaps simply, as one of the forgotten figures who served between two white-haired partisans, Thomas
P. O'Neill Jr. of Massachusetts and Newt Gingrich of Georgia.
Or perhaps poignantly, as the forlorn man who was toppled
from the giddiest heights of American politics . . . over a book.

Here, repetition binds the three supporting sentences tightly,
showing that each is a possibility. The repeated opening is especially effective for supporting sentences that could be arranged
in (almost) any order, as with *grandly*, *simply*, and *poignantly*,
though *poignantly* is the obvious finish.

Two more examples:

Crash. *Stockmarket bulls* can act as brave as they like but they
cannot deny the terror that this simple word strikes in their breasts.
They may reassure themselves with talk of record profits or the
death of inflation. They may point out all the ways in which
Wall Street's bull run is not like others which ended in tears. But
they cannot deny the stark reality: stockmarkets are notoriously
fickle and can turn against you at a moment's notice.

This book has three elements: *a description* of the terrible present state and future prospects of the American Economy, *a
theory* of the causes of the dreadful condition, *and a prescription* for rescuing us. The description of our condition is grossly
exaggerated. The theory of the causes of the alleged condition
is inadequately supported. The prescription is, with some ex-
ceptions, unpersuasive.

COUNT THE ELEMENTS

If you have two or three discrete details to support your point, your readers may absorb them better if they are counted.

This paragraph does not count the supporting sentences:

The stance and style of the inaugurals seem to have gone through some different phases. The phase that lasted until Lincoln was that of the modest, classic public servant. William Howard Taft marked the end of the phase of the prosaic government executive. We are still in the phase of the assertive, theatrical leader-preacher. This classification is not waterproof. Theodore Roosevelt may belong in the theatrical leader-preacher phase and Warren G. Harding–Calvin Coolidge–Herbert Hoover in the prosaic government executive phase. But the trend is clear.

How many phases were there? Not clear. Note the difference that counting can make:

The stance and style of the inaugurals seem to have gone through three phases. The first, lasting until Lincoln, was that of the modest, classic public servant. The second, lasting through William Howard Taft, was of the prosaic government executive. The third, in which we are still, is the phase of the assertive, theatrical leader-preacher. This classification is not waterproof. Theodore Roosevelt may belong in the third phase and Warren G. Harding–Calvin Coolidge–Herbert Hoover in the second. But the trend is clear.

Here are two more examples of counting:

Two durable impressions of the past two decades: first, women have made considerable progress in a short time in building human capabilities; and second, women have gone a considerable distance towards gender equality in education and health. These impressions are cause for hope, not pessimism, in the future.

Digitalization implies three things. First, that music can be faithfully recorded on a durable medium. That part has already happened, and saved the music business without changing it much. Second, that such recordings can be compressed and distributed in new ways. That is just beginning in America. Third, it implies that computers can speak the language of music.

SIGNAL WHAT'S TO COME

Revealing the relationships between sentences, transitional words can signal continuation *(and, further, furthermore, in addition, similarly),* reversal *(or, but, still, despite, otherwise, even so, nevertheless),* and conclusion *(so, thus, after all, in sum, in short, in brief).*

Here's a paragraph with no signals:

One of Mr. Blair's reasons for linking Britain and 2000 so closely is surely off the mark; strictly, the day begins at Greenwich, because it is at zero degrees of longitude, the meridian from which hours forward or back are conventionally reckoned. It is argued, the millennium will start in Britain. Tell that to the Russians, or to any of the majority of mankind that lives eastwards of Greenwich up to the International Date Line and whose midnight comes well before Britain's.

The paragraph makes sense, but the jump from the first sentence to the second is jarring and the remaining sentences are loose. Consider the following alternative, with signals:

Yet one of Mr. Blair's reasons for linking Britain with 2000 so closely is surely off the mark: strictly, the day begins at Greenwich, because it is at zero degrees of longitude, the meridian from which hours forward or back are conventionally reckoned. So, it is argued, the millennium will start in Britain. But tell that to the Russians, or indeed to any of the majority of mankind that lives eastwards of Greenwich up to the International Date Line and whose midnight comes well before Britain's.

Here are two more examples of deftly signaling what's to come:

Despite its one-sided arguments and hyperbolic claims, *The Great Betrayal* ought to stir discussion of such alternatives to the free-market internationalist status quo. Contrary to the best hopes of its advocates, the status quo has not extinguished the flames of nationalism but may actually be feeding them. If more of Buchanan's critics don't realize this soon, they may, ironically, end up leaving the stage to Buchanan himself.

This commercial dominance has been protected by a 10,000-strong private army, which has long fought off efforts by the central government in Yangon to bring it under control. As a result, Khun Sa is a rich man, with a lucrative market position to protect. So when, on New Year's Day, government troops walked unopposed into his headquarters at Ho Mong, it looked less like a military defeat, more as if the drug peddler had cut one more deal.

STICK TO ONE SUBJECT

If all the sentences in a paragraph are about one person, one idea, one country, try using the same noun or pronoun as the subject of each sentence.

Here is a paragraph with a new subject for each sentence:

In 1956 Endicott Peabody stood for election as attorney general of Massachusetts. Victory was not his. Next was a (failed)
run at the Democratic nomination for the governorship of
the state. Then the United States Senate candidacy—another
loss. Hence the move to New Hampshire, with unsuccessful
attempts for both houses of Congress. Endicott Peabody's
record of honourable failure was briefly interrupted in 1962
when, after a lengthy recount of the votes, he was elected governor of Massachusetts. But two years later defeat was again
the victor.

Compare that with *Endicott Peabody* as the subject for all sentences but one:

In 1956 Endicott Peabody stood for election as attorney general of Massachusetts. He lost. In 1958 he stood again, and
again lost. In 1960 he sought the Democratic nomination for
the governorship of the state, and failed. In 1966 he was a can-
didate for the United States Senate, and lost. In the 1980s he
moved to New Hampshire and tried for both houses of
Congress, but, sadly, lost again. Endicott Peabody's record of
honourable failure was briefly interrupted in 1962 when, after
a lengthy recount of the votes, he was elected governor of
Massachusetts. But two years later he was defeated.

The new subject of the next-to-the-last sentence works because
it signals Peabody's sole victory.

Two more examples:

Unbiased outsiders might blame languages, bad products and
state intervention. (Britain's music and publishing industries,
not hampered in these ways, compete head-to-head with

America's.) They might admit that Hollywood's libraries and worldwide distribution system give it a head start. But they would also note that when Europe produces films intended to please audiences as well as critics ("Four Weddings and a Funeral", for instance) it can do surprisingly well. And they would note too (as many in Hollywood do) that Tinseltown's bloated costs leave it surprisingly vulnerable to commercial competition. None of these thoughts has occurred to the lunatics running the EU's art asylum.

Gertrude Stein was not the stereotypical poor and alienated intellectual who was an enemy of capitalism. She always had a comfortable income, derived from her inheritance and supplemented after she turned 60 by her publishing royalties. She also had great investments—in Picassos, Matisses, and other paintings. Far from being alienated, she was the internationally recognized grande dame of a group of rising geniuses. And she was not an intellectual, having little interest in general ideas about economics or politics. "The real ideas," she said, "are not the relation of human beings as groups but a human being to himself inside him and that is an idea that is more interesting than humanity in groups."

Note how both paragraphs join equally weighted supporting sentences with *also* and *and*.

STICK TO ONE VERB FORM

Using one verb form rather than unnecessarily jumping from one form to another is always a good way to unify a paragraph.

The first paragraph uses a variety of verb forms, the second, only one.

Despite their stony homes, corals are fragile creatures. They will be crushed if you press too hard on them. If you cover them with silt, they can no longer feed on small passing animals. Blotting out the light by promoting the growth of algae in the waters above them would cause the other algae, with which they live symbiotically, to lose their ability to photosynthesize.

Despite their stony homes, corals are fragile creatures. Press too hard on them and they will be crushed. Cover them with silt and they can no longer feed on small passing animals. Blot out the light by promoting the growth of algae in the waters above them and other algae, with which they live symbiotically, can no longer photosynthesize.

The three imperatives of the second paragraph unify the three ideas loosely connected in the first.

In the next paragraph, the sentences are also similar in structure.

Ours cannot come out of the vision of any one man. It must be the product of the imaginations of many men. It must be a sharing with all peoples of our Bill of Rights, our Declaration of Independence, our Constitution, our magnificent industrial products, our technical skills. It must be an internationalism of the people, by the people and for the people.

FOLD TWO SENTENCES INTO ONE

Whenever two short sentences have the same subject, see whether you can fold one into the other—to show your reader which is the less important idea, which the more. Such folding is one of the easiest and most effective ways of picking up the pace of your paragraphs and tightening your sentences.

Compare this:

> Seven Japanese trust banks have "volunteered" to reduce the purchase of foreign securities by their pension funds. They have done this on orders from the ministry of finance.

with this:

> Seven Japanese trust banks, on orders from the ministry of finance, have "volunteered" to reduce the purchase of foreign securities by their pension funds.

This:

> These pension funds have been investing abroad more than 30% of their net intake of funds during the past seven months. They have been tempted by high interest rates and Wall Street's bull run.

with this:

> Tempted by high interest rates and Wall Street's bull run, these pension funds have been investing abroad more than 30% of their net intake of funds during the past seven months.

And this:

> Now they will cut overseas investment to 20%. They hope to reduce capital outflows and so to strengthen the yen.

with this:

> Now they will cut overseas investment to 20%, hoping to re-
> duce capital outflows and so to strengthen the yen.

For each of these three pairs of sentences, the writer subordi-
nated the less important idea to the more important by combin-
ing both in one sentence.

2

MAKE YOUR POINTS IN COMPELLING WAYS

FEW writers consider how or where to make a point in a paragraph. Most express the point in the first sentence and support it in subsequent sentences with details and examples. While effective, this construction becomes less so when it is overused, and more so when alternated with other ways of making a point. Deciding how to make your point depends on the details, examples, and comments you have to support it.

LEAD WITH THE POINT AND SUPPORT IT

The most common way to develop a paragraph is to state the point in the first sentence and support it, in subsequent sentences, with evidence: details, examples, and comments. When you lead with the point, your reader can identify it immediately, and a skimmer can pick up your line of argument by reading the first sentence of each paragraph. This form of development is what most of us use for two-thirds of our writing.

Motorists can be a lonely lot. They may get periodic traffic updates along with the news, chat and music from their car radios. With cell phones, they can even talk back to the outside world—asking for directions and apologising for being late. But, by and large, drivers are cut off more than most people from the torrent of information that pervades modern life. And it's a good thing, too, some might say.

After the point about secular trends, the second sentence identifies one trend and the third elaborates on it, while the fourth identifies another trend and the fifth, sixth, and seventh elaborate on it.

Here are two more paragraphs with leading points that are clearly supported in the sentences that follow them:

As big trees go, the baobab, Adansonia digitata, *is a whopper.* While it doesn't have the majestic height of North America's sequoia or the serpentine grandeur of Africa's red-leaved ficus, it has, well, presence. In fact, South Africa's bushmen believe the tree, some time after its creation, offended the gods, who then commanded it to grow upside down. And in the winter dry season, when the baobab loses its leaves, that's what it looks like—a massive, squat succulent, with its roots sticking up in the air.

In America, the second most important cause of increased income inequality has been a change in household structure. In the 1950s most households consisted of two parents, only one of whom was a wage-earner. Now society is more polarized between two-earner households and jobless single parent families. It is hard for single mothers to earn good incomes. The proportion of families headed by women among the poorest fifth of households has doubled over the past 40 years to around 35%. In contrast, the richest fifth of households is increasingly dominated by high-income two-earner couples: well-paid women tend to marry rich men.

LEAD WITH THE POINT AND CONCLUDE WITH A COMMENT

Concluding a paragraph with a comment can inject a bit of your personality and, at times, humor. Comments can also put a paragraph in perspective, create a bridge to the next paragraph, or reinforce your point after presenting a series of facts.

> *Geography is not geology, but they can be interlinked in surprising ways.* Geographically, Sakhalin Island is part of the Russian Far East, though half of it was Japanese territory until 1945. Geologically, though, it is a northward extension of Japan and thus prone to the same sort of seismic ups and downs as the rest of that archipelago. Earthquakes are no respectors of political boundaries.

> *Globally, the increasing stature of humans has untold environmental consequences.* Everyone knows that we need more energy and natural resources to meet the needs of the earth's population as it grows. But virtually no one thinks about the increasing needs of people who are growing taller and heavier. Larger human size is directly related to increased energy consumption. The hot water needs of the average household, for example, are a function of size; hot water needs for showers are body-surface-area related, baths are body-volume related. So a population of larger people puts increased demands on hot water heaters.

Try inserting a comment as a stand-alone fragment:

> *If Japan's banks dumped their bonds, long-term rates might rise, but short-term ones would fall.* No catastrophe, that.

as part of a sentence:

> *Mice whose RNA could not be edited developed epileptic seizures and died:* a heavy penalty for taking no notice of the editor.

or as a single word:

> Slyly, *they give "representational painting" an entirely new meaning.*

Gauge how much humor, irreverence, and personal opinion your readers will tolerate: don't make so many comments that they distract readers from your argument.

LEAD WITH THE POINT AND, USING CONJUNCTIONS, JOIN DETAILS

If you have, say, three supporting sentences of equal weight (none more important than the others), try linking them with *also* and *and* in the pattern shown here: *X is . . . , X is also . . . , and X is . . . .* By using these conjunctions and the same pronoun in each sentence, you can stress the equality or sequence of the details, pulling your readers through the paragraph.

> *At first sight the virtues of teamwork look obvious.* Teams make workers happier by giving them the feeling that they are shaping their own jobs. They also increase efficiency by eliminating layers of managers whose job was once to pass orders downwards. And, in principle, they enable a company to draw on the skills and imagination of a whole workforce, instead of relying on a specialist to watch out for mistakes and suggest improvements.

Germany is generous to immigrants. For a start, and in deference to their bloodline, it receives each year more than 200,000 Russians, the *Aussiedler* (outsettlers) whose German ancestors moved to Russia two centuries ago. On moral grounds, it takes in any Russian Jews who want to come. It has also admitted (in theory temporarily, though it may turn out permanently) more than half the entire outflow of refugees from the wars in the Balkans. And until three years ago, when it tightened its wide-open asylum laws, it received a good three-quarters of all third-world asylum-seekers reaching the European Union. Beyond that, it is home to some 2m Turkish immigrants originally taken in as "guest workers."

Note how this pattern strings the details together, injecting pace. The starting point is to look for details that start with—or could start with—the same subject and that appear to be of roughly equal importance. It works best if you have three details.

LEAD WITH THE POINT AND LIST DISPARATE DETAILS

Sometimes you can leave out such supporting conjunctions as *also* and *and* to add an edgy cadence to your details. Without conjunctions the series hits the reader in quick bursts, making each detail stand out. It also gives the impression that the list is not exhaustive.

Sierra Leone's post-dictatorship problems are almost absurd in their breadth. It once exported rice; now it can't feed itself. The life span of the average citizen is 39, the shortest in Africa. Unemployment stands at 87 percent and tuberculosis is spreading out of control. Corruption, brazen and ubiquitous, is a cancer on the economy.

Here the writer even leaves out the conjunction between the clauses of the first supporting sentence, joining them instead with a semicolon: *It once exported rice; now it can't feed itself.* Notice, too, how a consistent verb, *is*, binds the sentences of the paragraph.

Below, short sentences are even more staccato:

After a French winter of discontent, comes a hint of spring. The economy is starting to pick up. The seemingly inexorable rise in unemployment is slowing. Taxes, having reached a record high, are at last dropping. Interest rates are at their lowest level in 35 years. Trade is booming. Business morale is less flat. Even President Jacques Chirac and Alain Juppé, his Gaullist prime minister, are finally edging their way up from their previous abysmal depths in the opinion polls.

Supporting sentences made up of disparate details have different subjects. Since you are stripping the paragraph of its linking conjunctions, use all present-tense verbs or even the same verb to enhance cohesion. (For more on parallel structure, see "Stick to one subject," page 34, and "Stick to one verb form," page 36.) To try it, start with more than two details of equal weight. Short details work best. Pile them up. See what happens.

LEAD WITH THE POINT AND FOLLOW IT WITH A BULLETED LIST

A list of numerical facts, complicated details, or recommendations can be difficult for readers to lift off the page from a block of text. Breaking that block into bulleted items clarifies those elements and works well for setting up a line of argument.

Why do this?

- To articulate three, four, or more facts
- To relieve a dense block of text or a long series
- To set each element apart, making it easier to remember
- To highlight a list of recommendations or important ideas

The ratio of global trade to GDP has been rising over the past decade, but it has been falling for 44 developing countries, with more than a billion people. *The least developed countries,* with 10% of the world's people, *have only 0.3% of world trade*—half their share of two decades ago.

The list goes on:
- More than half of all developing countries have been bypassed by foreign direct investment, two-thirds of which has gone to only eight developing countries.
- Real commodity prices in the 1990s were 45% lower than those in the 1980s—and 10% lower than the lowest level during the Great Depression, reached in 1932.
- The terms of trade for the least developed countries have declined a cumulative 50% over the past 25 years.
- Average tariffs on industry country imports from the least developed countries are 30% higher than the global average.
- Developing countries lose about $60 billion a year from agricultural subsidies and barriers to textile exports in industrial nations.

If financial systems are to reach low-income female entrepreneurs and producers, delivery systems need to respond to the common characteristics of low-income women and their businesses:
- Women have less experience in dealing with formal financial institutions.
- Women tend to have smaller enterprises and fewer assets.
- Women are less likely to own land or other assets and face legal barriers to borrowing in many countries.

- Illiteracy rates are higher among women.
- Low-income women tend to concentrate on different economic activities than low-income men.

The trick to writing this kind of paragraph is knowing when *not* to do it. Some reports have bullets everywhere. Used too frequently, they lose their effectiveness and become an excuse for not writing complete paragraphs. That said, there are good reasons for using them: to organize many numerical facts or to emphasize important recommendations.

CONCLUDE WITH THE POINT AFTER INTRODUCING THE SUBJECT

Occasionally, put the point at the end of a paragraph to build suspense. Do this sparingly, however, because readers tire of having to wait for you to get to the point.

One way to conclude with the point: introduce a subject, discuss it, then make a point about it at the end.

For as long as humans have co-operated in meeting their material needs, they have been falling out over who gets what. Quarrels over distribution have always been part of the background noise of politics. Sometimes they have been much more than that. At certain points they have mounted in intensity and provoked a crisis, later subsiding as they were resolved or otherwise forgotten. The turning points in this cycle have marked some of the most traumatic events of human history. *If concerns over economic inequality are mounting once again, it is a matter of more than passing interest.*

Imagine that a mad scientist went back to 1950 and offered to transport the median family to the wondrous world of the

1990s, and to place them at, say, the 25th percentile level. The 25th percentile of 1996 is a clear material improvement over the median of 1950. Would they accept his offer? Almost surely not—because in 1950 they were middle class, while in 1996 they would be poor, even if they lived better in material terms. *People don't just care about their absolute material level, they care about their level compared with others.*

Although it may be tempting, resist the urge to impose this design on perfectly sound leading-point paragraphs just to add rhetorical interest. One good place to use a concluding-point paragraph is at the start of a piece. In this prime location, concluding-point paragraphs lead readers into a piece gently.

Another place to use this pattern is when you're trying to make a point that you know might be hard for your readers to swallow. By putting the point at the end, you allow time for a softening preface and give yourself a chance to explain your position.

CONCLUDE WITH THE POINT AFTER LISTING DISPARATE DETAILS

Another way to conclude with the point is to list disparate details and bring them together with a point at the end. The short bursts pile up somewhat mysteriously until the point, even the subject, is revealed at the end.

Black helicopters hover menacingly over Michigan; trains loaded with white UN trucks trundle across Oregon. Sinister? You bet: the onset of world government, no less. Or rather a sample of the nonsense that lands daily on a congressman's desk. After a bit, the congressman pays attention. He knows that the helicopters were American, flying low-level training missions; that the trucks were Canadian, destined for a UN mission; that the people who propagate this sort of stuff are nuts. *But behind the tall stories is something serious: the intense mistrust that some Americans feel for almost anything the UN does.*

You can see America wilting in downtown Silver Spring. Old office blocks stand empty. A grand art deco cinema is frequented only by ghosts. Glitzy department stores have decamped to out-of-town shopping malls. Tattoo parlours, pawnbrokers, discounters remain. This decay, multiplied a thousand times in towns across America, is especially painful in a country built on the idea of progress. Lacking a common history, ethnicity, or even language, *Americans are held together by a singular optimism: by the American dream.*

Too colorful for some pieces, obviously inappropriate for others, this pattern can puzzle your readers, so be sure the details are vivid enough to intrigue them. If readers don't make it to the end of the paragraph, they will not get to your point.

Writing this kind of paragraph can take practice. If you have a series of powerful, descriptive details, try stringing them together. If you like the results but the effect is dubious, you might want to make the point at the beginning (see "Lead with the point and list disparate details," page 44).

The other thing to consider is your subject. This structure often works well for controversial points because as the details unfold, your readers become curious and follow along in the deduction.

MAKE THE POINT IN THE MIDDLE

Sometimes, though not often, your point is best put in the middle of the paragraph. The first few sentences of the paragraph introduce the (perhaps surprising) point and soften its arrival.

Amber is fossil resin, the consequence of tree injuries suffered millions of years ago. Its early significance to science can be seen from its ancient Greek name—elektron. Until the invention of batteries, rubbing amber was the best-known way of generating (static) electricity. *But amber's modern importance to science is as a trap.* Hundreds of species of ancient creepy-crawly are known to paleontologists only because they blundered into a blob of resin many million years ago. David Grimaldi, a curator whose fascination with amber led to the museum's global search for exhibits and treasures, says that amber's paleontological role is much misunderstood, thanks largely to its appearance in "Jurassic Park."

In the paragraph above, the first three sentences inform readers about amber's historical importance, which sets up a comparison with amber's significance today.

The first few sentences of the paragraph below establish the writer's position and provide background to the point:

Among the many convenient targets that Republican politicians and intellectuals have at their disposal, the one at which they direct their fire with perhaps the most delight is the academy. George Will, William Bennett, and other right-wing thinkers never tire of recounting the follies of professors and of portraying them as naive, duped, and possibly duplicitous. *The right has made especially clever and effective use of the widespread suspicion of multiculturalism.* A large portion of the American middle class has been made to believe that the universities are under the control of a "political correctness" police. This false belief has made it easier for the racists, the sexists, and the homophobes to dismiss their opponents as far-out, self-intoxicated radicals—out of touch with the sound common sense of mainstream America.

To build this kind of paragraph, try folding a paragraph with a strong point into a more general opening or introductory paragraph. Remember that you are placing an important sentence in the least conspicuous place, so be sure that the point is strong enough to stand out—even if you're trying to soften it.

UNDERMINE A PREMISE AT THE END OF THE PARAGRAPH

Undermining an idea is a clever way to make your point stand out while taking the claws out of an opposing view. The decision about undermining at the beginning, middle, or end of a paragraph depends on how much information you want to give in support of the premise.

Undermining at the end of a paragraph is like concluding with the point—but in a backhanded way. It shows your understanding of an alternative point of view—then slams the direction of the argument into reverse.

Undermining can:

• highlight an opponent's flaws or weaknesses
• present (and refute) a common misconception
• introduce tension or create the atmosphere of debate.

It is widely believed, especially by labor union officials, that the fall of the blue collar industrial worker in the developed countries was largely, if not entirely, caused by moving production "offshore" to countries with abundant supplies of unskilled labor and low wage rates. *But this is not true.*

In the above example, your readers have an immediate clue that you don't agree with the premise *(It is widely believed)*. The strong statement at the end *(But this is not true)* leaves no doubt about your position, presumably to be elaborated in the following paragraph.

Here is another paragraph that undermines the opening point at the end:

> Whenever an attempt is made to marry economics with Charles Darwin, it is well to raise a sceptical eyebrow. And the case for scepticism is all the stronger when natural selection is invoked to explain some pattern of things which, pretty clearly, could be changed by a simple act of will. For many years it has been argued that the present shape of the American corporation, in which a vast and dispersed group of shareholders exercises little or no control over the firm's managers, is in some way preordained. Organising firms like this, runs the argument, is simply the most efficient way of adapting to the demands of modern capitalism. *This view has its alluring points, but is wrong.*

Think of a premise you disagree with, opening it with a phrase like:

- *It is widely believed*
- *Many people think*
- *It may seem*
- *At first glance*

Then give the reader a few details about the premise, details that you can later turn to your advantage as you support your points. Along the way, you might intersperse such phrases as "it is argued" and "so goes the argument," to remind readers that you are not presenting your own view. Last, shift the direction of the argument by undermining the premise, perhaps signaling the shift with:

- *Yet*
- *But*
- *Actually*
- *A closer look reveals*
- *On the contrary*

UNDERMINE A PREMISE IMMEDIATELY

Sometimes, you may not need to elaborate on the premise you intend to debunk, allowing you to attack it immediately.

> But capital gains are special, the engines of entrepreneurship and growth. *No. There is nothing special about capital gains.* Simple accounting alchemy can turn almost any form of income into a capital gain, and will do so if the tax rate is different enough. Capital gains are often—but not always—the reward for risk taking, whereas dividends and interest are usually the payoff of safer investments. And risk taking is swell. But the market will reward a higher risk with a higher payoff—if the risk makes sense, and if you believe in the market.

> The point is well taken; *it is also misleading.* The issue is not the difficulty of writing but the fetishizing of difficulty, the belief that fractured English, name dropping, and abstractions guarantee profundity, professionalization, and subversion. With this belief comes the counter-belief: lucidity implies banality, amateurism, capitalism, and conservatism.

Undermining immediately is more abrupt than undermining at the end. Its quick shift can also be used as a transition between paragraphs (see "Link your paragraphs," pages 66–83).

UNDERMINE A PREMISE IN THE MIDDLE OF THE PARAGRAPH

Undermining a premise after you've given readers some background allows you to fit the whole process (state premise, support it, undermine it with a point, support point) into one paragraph. That, however, can make for long paragraphs.

Chroniclers of the rise of the industrial worker tend to highlight the violent episodes—especially the clashes between strikers and the police, as in America's Pullman strike. The reason is probably that the theoreticians and propagandists of socialism, anarchism, and communism—beginning with Marx and continuing to Herbert Marcuse in the 1960s—incessantly wrote and talked of "revolution" and "violence." *Actually, the rise of the industrial worker was remarkably nonviolent.* The enormous violence of this century—the world wars, ethnic cleansings, and so on—was all violence from above rather than violence from below; and it was unconnected with the transformation of society, whether the dwindling of farmers, the disappearance of domestic servants, or the rise of the industrial worker. In fact, no one even tries anymore to explain these great convulsions as part of the "crisis of capitalism," as was standard Marxist rhetoric only thirty years ago.

At first glance, it may seem absurd to propose that the cash visible in the capital is symptomatic of things getting better elsewhere across Russia. During the past four years industrial production has halved (America's fell by less than a third during the Depression). *Government data, however, give cause for guarded optimism.* The decline in industrial output may have bottomed out; output has been steady for the past three months; living standards have actually improved. According to Goskomstat, the official collector of statistics, real (i.e., adjusted for inflation) household incomes rose by 18% in the year to July, and real household consumption by 10%. There are also signs of changes in the pattern of consumption: imports of chicken and red meat rose from 90,000 tonnes in January to 399,000 tonnes in August. Critics of reform will complain that Russia cannot afford to live on imported food — yet, in the first eight months of this year, Russia had a trade surplus of 11.7 billion.

To break these paragraphs up, you could put all the supporting sentences into a separate paragraph.

START WITH A QUESTION AND ANSWER IT IMMEDIATELY

Asking a question in the first line of a paragraph grabs readers' attention and sets up your point. Using an immediate, direct answer to make your point demonstrates a firm stance, emphasized by the confidence of a fragment.

Perhaps heightism is just a western cultural prejudice? *Sadly not.* In Chinese surveys, young women always rate stature high among qualifications for a future mate. Indeed, the prejudice appears to be universal.

So will squash eventually rival tennis as a spectator sport, and will Jansher Khan and Peter Marshall become as rich and famous as Pete Sampras and Andre Agassi? *Almost certainly not.*

For all the gimmicks of a glasswalled court, a special white ball and more and better cameras, squash remains fearsomely difficult to televise. Not only does the ball move too fast but the camera lens foreshortens the action. Squash, therefore, is destined to remain a sport better played than watched. Given its propensity for what the tennis authorities term "audible obscenities", that may be just as well.

Immediate answers make you seem—merely seem—unequivocal. They also engage your readers with a conversational tone. And they don't leave the answer to the reader.

An indirect answer is less firm. In the next paragraph, the writer avoids offending anybody by slithering:

Can the euro still be stopped? In Germany, both a driving force behind a single European currency and home to the biggest contingent of sceptics, a last-minute bid to delay its introduction has drawn ridicule from the government. "I am as sure [the euro] will be launched as I am of hearing 'Amen' in church," said the foreign minister, Klaus Kinkel. Maybe, if he does not get caught in the traffic that is building up alarmingly en route.

The next paragraph also ends with a question, throwing the first point into doubt and providing a transition to the paragraph that follows it:

Why is Dylan [Thomas's] legacy so ambivalent? *His reputation for being a drunk sits uneasily amid the Methodist chapels of South Wales.* When Dylan's Bookshop opened in the town 25 years ago, old men would come in, stare at the first editions and other memorabilia, and exclaim: "I knew him, the bloody waster." But was it entirely true?

Whether answered directly or indirectly, questions bring your readers closer to the text by making them feel part of the discourse. Compare this point:

Our current system of teaching and learning is not very effective.

with this one:

How effective is our current system of teaching and learning? Not very.

A question and immediate answer can thus make a flat point more arresting.

START WITH A QUESTION AND ANSWER IT IN SUCCEEDING SENTENCES

If the question defies a simple, straightforward answer, answer it in several sentences. You will still grab your audience's attention with an opening question but will reveal the answer more slowly.

This form works well for setting up a complicated or involved point, or for suggesting a point without stating it directly.

So *why is the countryside booming?* Agricultural growth accelerated in the 1980s; roads and electricity reached most villages in the 1980s, helping start new businesses in transport and construction as well as manufacturing. The spread of electricity has raised productivity in the countryside, as well as increasing rural demand for electrically driven gadgets. As electricity has spread television, so television has presented India's villagers with the joys of the consuming life.

So *how can you tell if a Halls cough drop is too old?* After two years, the cough drop begins to look cloudy, it becomes softer and stickier, loses shape and begins to "flow into the cracks and crevices" of its wrapper, a Warner-Lambert spokesman says. Though the drops essentially contain the properties of hard candy, the company says the lozenges lose their effectiveness after about two and a half years.

In both paragraphs, the opening questions give the reader a lens for focusing on the sentences that follow.

START WITH A QUESTION AND ANSWER IT AT THE END

When you want to explore several possibilities or give reasons before answering a question, try putting the answer at the end of the paragraph. The effect is to make you seem thoughtful, thorough, cautious.

This kind of paragraph is similar to one that concludes with the point after introducing the subject (page 47). And here, too, be sure you don't lose your reader before arriving at your point—in this case, the answer to the opening question.

How many ideas—and how much fact—can a novel contain before it begins to turn into something else altogether—a work of non-fiction, for instance? Some famous examples spring to mind. The Napoleonic armies marched right the way through Tolstoy's epic "War and Peace" without protest from the author. One of the 18th century's best works of fiction, Laurence Sterne's "Tristram Shandy," was also one of the oddest novels ever written—part eccentric autobiography and part an examination of the nature of time. Closer to our own day, Norman Mailer fashioned his greatest novel, "The Executioner's Song," from the gruesome lineaments of a mass-murderer called Gary Gilmore. So how much can a novelist get away with? *It entirely depends upon whether or not he can sustain our interest by sheer force of persuasive imaginative skill.*

Why did the highly paid economists in the investment banks and the international financial institutions fail to predict the crisis? The IMF did issue several warnings to Thailand during the year before the collapse, but the government ignored it. *The handful of economists who rang alarm bells,* such as Jim Walker at Crédit Lyonnais and Mark McFarland at Peregrine Securities, *were generally thought to be too gloomy.*

In the first paragraph, the writer sets out three examples, re-states the question, and then gives the answer to make the paragraph's point. In the second paragraph, the writer gives one answer immediately, undermines it, and concludes with the point, nicely sandwiching the supportive details.

ASK SEVERAL QUESTIONS AND ANSWER EACH IMMEDIATELY

A series of answered questions can give a paragraph a bantering, argumentative tone. And if you know your readers are going to have questions about the point you are making, try asking the questions yourself so that you can address each of them directly.

But which countries should represent these regions. India? Pakistan says no. Brazil? Argentina says no. Nigeria? Everybody says no. *Solutions galore have been suggested:* rotating members, tenured members, first-, second- and third-rank members, members without veto power, dropping the veto altogether or promising to use it in exceptional circumstances only.

You may say that the wretched of the earth should not be forced to serve as hewers of wood, drawers of water, and sewers of sneakers for the affluent. But what is the alternative? Should they be helped with foreign aid? Maybe—although the historical record of regions like southern Italy suggest that such aid has a tendency to promote perpetual dependence. Anyway, there isn't the slightest prospect of significant aid materializing. Should their own governments provide more social justice? Of course—but they won't, or at least, not because we tell them to. And as long as you have no realistic alternative to industrialization based on low wages, *to oppose it means that you are willing to deny desperately poor people the best chance they have of progress for the sake of what amounts to an aesthetic standard*—that is, the fact that you don't like the idea of workers being paid a pittance to supply rich Westerners with fashion items.

In the first paragraph, the writer uses questions to bring up and shoot down three possibilities, conveying the difficulties of reaching a consensus. In the second paragraph, the writer uses questions to open a conversation.

IMPLY THE POINT IN A SERIES OF DETAILS OR EXAMPLES

Most writers imply too many of their points—which their readers, bewildered, fail to infer. But having one point-led paragraph after another can get monotonous. So, when it's really possible to get a point across without stating it, give your reader some relief—and credit for being able to figure things out.

For one thing, Milan is shrinking—the population has fallen from 1.6m in 1981 to 1.3m today. The economy, which boomed in the 1980s, is dozier. Unemployment, now 8%, has been rising. In 1994–95, the number of businesses rose by only 2%, compared with 35% for Italy as a whole. Although Milan is home to five good universities and has far more head offices of multinationals than any other city in Italy, it is struggling to attract new blood. Even in areas of traditional strength—fashion, banking, publishing, advertising and high technology—Milan is losing its grip. Buildings once started seem to remain unfinished for ever. Prostitution is spreading.

Point: Milan is losing its power economically and intellectually.

[Meteorite] specimens prized for their beauty or rare composition can sell for more than $500 a gram (barely one twenty-eighth of an ounce), while meteorites from Mars, only 12 of which are known to have been recovered, go for more than $1,000 a gram. Mr. Killgore's daily harvest on a recent trip to the Chilean desert was $2,000 in meteorite nuggets.

Point: Meteorite specimens are rising in value.

This kind of paragraph needs strong details to hold it up. The point should begin to be obvious in the first or second detail and should be confirmed by the rest—don't keep your reader guessing.

If the details cannot stand on their own, you can easily make the point explicit and put it at the beginning or the end.

IMPLY THE POINT IN A SERIES OF QUESTIONS

Turning everything into a question emphasizes the unknown elements of an issue and gives a paragraph a sense of insistence. The questions can express frustration or concern. They can also plant doubt, hope, or curiosity. And they can highlight the many sides of an issue.

Keep in mind, though, that questions unanswered generally

leave your reader anxious—just as an unresolved chord would. So, one good use of this pattern is in the opening of a piece, to set up questions that you will discuss and answer later.

> But if there is indeed a connection between population and conflict, how does it work? What is its "operational chemistry"? Do population problems directly and inevitably lead to violence? Or do they work indirectly, for example, in catalytic conjunction with other factors such as environmental decline? If the latter, does the "other-factor" complication make population itself less potent as a source of conflict? Or does it make it all the more dangerous, in that population pressures then work in less overt, and hence less heeded, fashion?

Other times, the questions may be merely questioning, rhetorically:

> Should the UN still be trying to put the world to rights? Should it concentrate on social justice? Should it intervene in the civil conflicts that have become more common than wars between states? Should it curl up and die? And, if it is to lead an active life, how can it, when the poor thing is both despised and broke, its major debtors either refusing (the U.S.), or unable (Russia), to pay their bills?

And still other times, the series can support (quite explicitly) the opening point:

> How did things break down? What public ethics reign in a land whose police can kill 111 inmates in a raid on a security prison—and none of the policemen goes to jail, while ten are promoted? Where the head of the tax department has to resign for daring to levy duty on the 17 tons of booty brought back by Brazil footballers last summer with the newly won World Cup?

Where a state governor can walk into a restaurant, shoot his rival, walk away to applause, and win a Senate seat by a landslide? Where society gasps when the president watches carnival arm-in-arm with a semiclad samba dancer, but barely cares that the box he sat in belongs to racketeers?

As these paragraphs show, implication doesn't necessarily mean subtlety. Used occasionally, the pattern can be powerful.

IMPLY THE POINT BY PRESENTING TWO SIDES

Sometimes you may want to present two sides without taking a stand—either because of ignorance or diplomacy. You might also do this to suggest the complexity of a debate, thus allowing you

- to set up your point (choosing one side) in the following paragraph
- to avoid alienating readers when discussing a sensitive issue.

Not many people know it, but India is sitting on a mountain of 30m tonnes of grain; it could increase to 36m tonnes by the end of June, when the wheat harvest ends. *The sceptics say* this merely shows that the poor can no longer afford to buy grain, which is 60% dearer than it was when India started its economic liberalization in 1991. *The supporters of reform retort* that, reform having made many people richer, they are changing their eating habits and switching from cereals to superior foods such as meat, eggs, milk, and vegetables.

Should trade barriers be lowered before, or after, enterprises have been restructured? *Before, say those* who argue that the sudden introduction of freer trade offers domestic monopolies competition from abroad and introduces world prices, helping to correct the price distortions inherited from central planning. *After, say those* who argue that the introduction of foreign competition, though necessary, can be too sudden to allow lumbering domestic enterprises to adjust, threatening a general collapse of output and employment like that seen in East Germany. Poland lowered barriers quickly and now has one of the lowest tariff regimes in the world. Czechoslovakia and Hungary have eliminated most import quotas, though they have retained high tariffs on some products.

In both examples, an issue is presented in the first sentence and then interpreted in two ways. Notice that neither writer signals which side will be taken.

IMPLY THE POINT IN AN ANALOGY OR SYLLOGISM

Analogies and syllogisms can make a topic more engaging. In analogies, A is likened to B: *money* to *water*, *servant* to *financial servant*, and *master* to *industrial master*.

Money is like a body of *water*; a pebble dropped in here, a sluice gate opened there, can send ripples or waves that erode coastlines or flood cities far away. Junk bonds and hostile takeovers are mechanisms and outcomes rather than causes in themselves; building sea walls against them will not deal with their origins. The water will find other ways to transmit the forces which it is carrying.

No man is a hero to his valet: the close and obedient *servant* sees all the weaknesses and vulnerabilities of his *master*. So it is with the *financial servant* and its *industrial master*. Weaknesses in industry and in its political, legal, and social surroundings are observed by the financial system in their finest detail. Worst of all, finance is less discreet than the valet. It passes on its master's frailties for all to see.

More complicated, a syllogism likens A to B, B to C, and thus A to C.

All the *conversational devices* of economics, whether words or numbers, may be viewed as *figures of speech*. They are all metaphors, analogies, ironies, appeals to authority. *Figures of speech* are not mere frills. They *think for us*. Someone who thinks of a market as an "invisible hand" and the organization of work as a "production function" and coefficients as being "significant," as an economist does, is giving the language a great deal of responsibility. It seems a good idea to look hard at this language.

Here the writer has likened *conversational devices of economics* to *figures of speech,* and *figures of speech* (not *mere frills*) to [*things that*] *think for us.*

3

LINK YOUR PARAGRAPHS

Many of the devices that bind sentences within a paragraph—repeating a key term, counting the elements, signaling what's to come, asking and answering questions—can do the same work across paragraphs, creating smooth transitions from one to the next.

REPEAT A WORD OR PHRASE FROM THE END OF THE PRECEDING PARAGRAPH

Words or phrases from one paragraph repeated at the start of the next explicitly tie the two together.

Only 3,100 surnames are now in use in China, say researchers, compared with nearly 12,000 in the past. An "evolutionary dwindling" of surnames is common to all societies, according to Du Ruofu of the Chinese Academy of Sciences; but in China, he says, where surnames have been in use far longer than in most other places, *the paucity has become acute.*

To get an idea of just how *acute,* imagine that the combined populations of the United States and Japan had to make do with but five surnames. That, essentially, is how things are in China, where the five most common surnames—Li, Wang, Zhang, Liu, and Chen—are shared by no fewer than 350 million people. Those named Li alone number 87 million, nearly 8% of the country's Han people, the ethnic Chinese. Another 19 surnames each cover 1% or more of the population.

So far, RNA editing has been seen in marsupials, protozoa, slime moulds, ferns, and flowering plants. Flies *do it*. Mice *do it*. And, it now appears, people *do it*.

Or rather, in most cases, their mitochondria do it. Mitochondria—the cellular machines where glucose is burned for energy—are found in all cells more sophisticated than bacteria. Indeed, many biologists suspect that the ancestors of mitochondria actually were bacteria which gave up an independent life to live symbiotically in early complex cells. They have their own genes, in any case. And these genes are turning out be heavily edited.

TURN THE REPEATED WORD INTO A QUESTION

Turning the repeated word or phrase at the start of the second paragraph into a question raises an eyebrow of doubt or irony.

Many of the EFF's critics predicted this from the start. The move to Washington in the first place was fiercely controversial among its on-line constituency, whose members worried that the organization would lose touch with its *cultural roots*.

Cultural roots? It may be hard to imagine something as amorphous and all-included as cyberspace having either roots or a culture. But it does. The chief principle of this culture—decentralization—comes from the structure of the Internet, at present cyberspace's main incarnation. The Internet has no real governing body, no real shape, and almost no rules. It is nothing more than a common language by which computers can talk to each other.

In a country with no more arable land than Holland, Egypt has close on 60m people, half of them under 21. True, Egypt's economic indicators are bright—"a *vibrant* economy" is the current official phrase—but economists reckon that it would take a sustained growth rate of 7% or more to soak up the new job-seekers.

Vibrant? With the help of American development aid, parts of the country's infrastructure have been transformed: the telephones miraculously work, there is an electricity surplus, and a new metro system may, eventually, ease serious permanent traffic jams. But investors in Egypt have still to plough through a hideous quagmire of laws, regulations and bureaucracy.

Note how the second paragraphs, without the questions, would have a flat start. The questions thus link the paragraphs and enliven the prose.

REPEAT AN OPENING WORD OR PHRASE

Repeating an opening word or phrase at the beginning of paragraphs propels your argument across two or more of them.

Banks' *credit-risk models* are mind-bogglingly complex. But the question they try to answer is actually quite simple: how much of a bank's lending might plausibly turn bad? Armed with the answer, banks can set aside enough capital to make sure they stay solvent should the worst happen.

No model, of course can take account of every possibility.

Credit-risk models try to put a value on how much a bank should realistically expect to lose in the 99.9% or so of the time that passes for normality. This requires estimating three different things: the likelihood that any given borrower will default; the amount that might be recoverable if that happened; and the likelihood that the borrower will default at the same time others are doing so.

The repeated opening also tells readers that the paragraphs are doing similar work — that the second paragraph adds to or elaborates on the point of the first.

Small wonder, then, that such a variety of insects and plants were unwittingly trapped in the stickiness and thereby preserved, fragmentary DNA and all. The exhibition's 200-odd fossil marvels include entombed ants, a frog, a scorpion, a perfect flower and a yet-to-be-revealed mystery item that Dr Grimaldi discovered recently in New Jersey.

Small wonder, too, that amber has long had cultural significance. Though not especially rare (many trees exuded great gouts of the stuff) it is both attractive and easy to work. Amber has been carved since the Stone Age into symbolic figures and used as currency. The Greeks and Romans alike were fascinated by its weightless luminosity. In recent years the Baltic amber that was expensively transported across Europe to the Mediterranean 2,000 years ago has become ubiquitous as a cheap jewel, exported now as earrings and brooches by modern Balts as desperate as their forebears for trade.

SIGNAL WHAT'S TO COME

Conjunctions and transitional phrases join paragraphs by signaling reversals, continuations, and restatements.

Some of this hand-wringing is disingenuous. Many trade group lobbyists are privately crowing over having outflanked the Administration and the Democratic leadership; the National Federation of Independent Business Inc. (NFIB) send journalists reprints of a *U.S. News & World Report* article touting the small-business lobby's routing of reform legislation.

Nor should the lobbyist's somber demeanor be confused with regret. Most health care industry groups supported only narrow reform proposals of their own design and they clearly preferred inaction to any plan that threatened their members' livelihoods.

But the aftermath of the health care reform battle is unfolding like a bad mystery novel. The victim had dozens of enemies, but now that he's dead, all of them are finding something nice to say about him—and working hard on their alibis. Opinion polls show the public still clamoring for some type of reform, and no group wants to be the target of wrath for this year's inaction.

And gloating isn't a good way to win friends and influence people on Capitol Hill. House Energy and Commerce Committee chairman John D. Dinglee, D-Mich., has promised to hold extensive hearings into the operations of the insurance industry next year—giving a hint of the strained relationships left in the wake of this year's battle.

The best laid plans for the European Union's single currency may yet go astray, but at least the blueprint is on the table. On May 31 the European Commission released its ideas for economic and monetary union (EMU), and proposed a publicity blitz to gain popular support for a three-phase program: the decision to launch the single currency and identify the countries qualified to use it; the "irrevocable" fixing, within a deadline of the following 12 months, of the parities of those countries' currencies; and, within a deadline of three years after that, the transition to the single currency, with its coins and notes introduced "over a few weeks at the most".

In other words, read the Maastricht treaty, which gives starting dates for EMU of 1997 at the earliest and January 1st 1999 at the latest, add a year and then another three, and by 2003 Europeans will be emptying their pockets of marks and francs and filling them with a new Euro-currency.

Though many writers avoid opening a paragraph with a conjunction, as the writer of the second example does, these words are ideal transitional words—they are clear and direct, and tell readers what to expect next.

ESTABLISH PAIRS ACROSS PARAGRAPHS

Similar to repeating a word or phrase, mirroring elements from one paragraph to the next not only aids transition, but links the point of one paragraph to the next.

CIA officials used to have all sorts of irritating habits. If offered a perfectly good *Chateauneuf-du-Pape* at a Georgetown dinner party, they would praise it—by stressing their dissent from the "universal opinion" that unblended reds are better. If told of an especially good *trattoria* in Rome, they might express much gratitude for the information—and deplore their own laziness in always going to the same old Sabatini they had first encountered while vacationing in Italy with their parents. Even more irritating was the propensity of first-generation CIA officials for interjecting into any remotely relevant conversation memories of Groton, Yale, or skiing holidays in St. Moritz.

There is none of that sort of thing anymore. Today's CIA people are not wine snobs—in fact, many of them prefer beer, while others refrain from even coffee, as befits good Mormons. Nor are they partial to foreign foods in funky *trattorias*—

cheeseburgers are more their style. Instead of being Ivy League showoffs, they are quietly proud of their state colleges, however obscure these might be.

What people drink, where they eat, and where they went to school make the point about how CIA officials have changed.

ASK A QUESTION AT THE END OF ONE PARAGRAPH AND ANSWER IT AT THE BEGINNING OF THE NEXT

Questions suggest answers. Posing a question at the end of a paragraph signals the reader to look for your answer in the next.

> Having to announce a big drop in profits is not the way any chairman would choose to mark his second week on the job. That was the unenviable task of the new chief of J.P. Morgan, one of America's oldest and mightiest banks, on January 12. Douglas Warner disclosed that the bank's net profit in 1994 was $1.2 billion, 29% less than in 1993. *So why does he look so cheerful?*
>
> *Perhaps because he thinks the bank's hardest work has been done.* Morgan is at the tail end of a metamorphosis that started in the late 1970s, when this starched commercial bank saw big corporate borrowers turning in their masses from bank loans toward cheaper sources of capital, such as bonds. Under the chairmanship of Sir Dennis Weatherstone, Morgan changed further, concentrating resources on the fee-earning businesses, such as advising clients, and on trading securities. By the end of 1993, noninterest income accounted for 72% of Morgan's earnings, compared with 39% a decade earlier.

A bare two years before the ceremonial opening of St Peter's Holy Door hails the new millennium, Romans are scratching their heads. How can the eternal city cope with an expected influx of millions? Will the traffic flow? Can Rome, even with help from central coffers, afford the sort of projects that the jubilee's organizers deem essential? *Will they, budgets willing, be ready on time?*

Do not bet on it. The space problem is the oldest and worst. For hundreds of years, fragile old Rome has been hard put to embrace a few hundred thousand pilgrims—let alone the 20m–40m expected in the millennial year. Rome lacks vast open spaces. The Piazza San Giovanni, the city's biggest, is chock-full with about 170,000 people; Piazza del Popolo can hold a mere 62,000.

In the second example, a flood of questions gets a simple answer at the start of the second paragraph, quickly dismissing any possibility that Rome might cope.

ASK A QUESTION AT THE BEGINNING OF THE SECOND PARAGRAPH

Opening with a question about the previous paragraph announces that an explanation will follow.

Platinum may be more expensive, troy ounce for troy ounce, but gold remains the noblest metal in the eyes of chemists. Other so-called noble metals react fairly easily with their environment—a copper roof turns green and silver tarnishes—but gold's ability to resist all but the strongest acids is part of the reason it has fascinated kings and commoners for centuries. Even platinum helps other chemicals to react, which is why it is used as a catalyst for car exhausts. Gold, however, remains haughtily above such common tasks, refusing to react with the molecular masses.

But why? It is not as though gold were chemically inert. After all, anything less than 24-carat gold is an example of gold's ability to bond strongly with other noble metals. The unresolved puzzle has been why oxygen, hydrogen, and other reactive constituents of the atmosphere—and the constituents of many acids—are hard put to bond with gold. Theorists in Denmark now believe that they have the answer. And their calculations do not only provide an explanation for gold's unique pedigree. They also point the way to designing better catalysts.

In other cases, families can afford to send their children to school only if they also work at the same time. It is this family dilemma that makes laws against child labor so difficult to enforce. Thus in Mexico children obtain forged birth certificates in order to secure jobs in the maquiladora factories operated by U.S. firms along the northern border. And it is this that makes worthy corporate codes of conduct liable to backfire: the danger is that, far from contributing to the end of child labor, they merely shift it to shadier areas of the economy that are far harder to police.

So what should companies do? Some initiatives appear more promising than others. One such is the effort that Levi Strauss, a maker of jeans, has made to provide schooling for child workers in its suppliers' plants in Bangladesh. The provision of other benefits, such as medical care and meals, may also be appropriate.

The *Börsen-Zeitung* is among the most expensive daily papers in the world. For the hefty DM 7.20 ($3.80) cover price, readers get the best and most detailed reporting of German companies. The editor, Hans Konradin Herdt, has the sharpest pen of any financial journalist in the country: bound copies of his leading articles are sent to all subscribers as a Christmas present. His satirical talents reduce sober-sided German financiers to stitches. "A silver bullet into the boardroom," is one advertiser's assessment of the paper's reach.

Just who reads it? That, it turns out, is a closely guarded secret. Usually for a newspaper supported by advertising, the *Börsen-Zeitung* refuses to disclose figures, lest they be "misunderstood," Mr. Herdt says. It also declines to commission standard research about its jobs and spending power. Insiders suspect that circulation is small, between 6,000 and 10,000. Simon McPhillips of DMB&B, an advertising agency, says the "ludicrous" lack of information certainly deters advertisers, especially foreign ones.

MAKE A COMMENT

Opening comments—like opening questions—strengthen the link with the preceding paragraph.

Austria, Finland, and Sweden have joined the club. The new members will do no more than tilt the map of Europe a bit to the north and east, but that is proving enough to make those on the southern fringes feel uneasy. They are worried that their concerns will seem relatively unimportant to the northern majority. In particular they fret about North Africa.

With good reason. The Christmas hijacking of an Air France jet by Islamic extremists served as a grim reminder to the French that their former colony, Algeria, is fighting a civil war that may well spill over into France and prompt an exodus of refugees across the Mediterranean. Like France, Spain and Italy already receive a steady flow of illegal immigrants from North Africa, where poverty and fecundity combine to make the adventurous seek a better life in Europe.

Sanctions have recently come to seem the tool of choice in foreign policy. During the cold war, the big task of containing communism was done mainly with tanks and nukes: from 1945 until the break-up of the Soviet Union in 1991, America imposed sanctions less than once a year on average. Now, deprived of a single overarching threat, Americans worry about a range of lesser ones. Few warrant the use of force; all exercise some Washington constituency enough to generate pressure for action. And so, on Mr. Eizenstat's count, America resorted to sanctions 61 times between 1993 and 1996—a frequency 15 times greater than during the cold war.

Up to a point, this is fine. In the past, western sanctions risked driving private countries into the arms of the Soviet Bloc; these days, Russia can be persuaded to go along with sanctions on pariahs like Iraq, so they are more effective. But the rise of sanctions also reflects troubling trends.

The comments—*With good reason* and *Up to a point, this is fine*—could have been made at the end of the first paragraph, but that would have broken the link with the second.

COUNT

Counting is a simple but effective transitional device to link several paragraphs.

However, there are several reasons why the government should be cautious before dipping its hands into taxpayers' pockets. *First,* although charities seem to add significant value at current levels of funding, there is no guarantee that any extra money will produce similar amounts of added value. It may be that charities' income and outputs are around their optimal level, and that the value added would fall as their income, and therefore their costs, rose.

Second, the study does not look at whether the government agencies or private firms could perform good works more efficiently than charities do. In research comparing care homes for the elderly, Laing & Buisson, a health-care consultancy, has found that charity-run homes are less cost-effective than ones run by for-profit firms. Were this true of good deeds in general, it might be better for the government to hire private contractors to care for vulnerable people, instead of subsiding charities to do so.

First and above all, the "Decline and Fall" is a good history. In its massive erudition, its phenomenal accuracy and its sober judgment it still stands as the indispensable starting point of any study of the Roman empire. *Second*, the work should be read for the majesty of Gibbon's prose. This is eloquence in the grandest manners, cunningly matched to its twin functions of narration and explanation. It is not to be imitated, but to be studied and enjoyed.

PLACE PARAGRAPHS IN TIME

When your paragraphs show a progression in time, use that natural chronology to link them.

In 1969, when relations between China and the Soviet Union were at their worst, China provoked a series of skirmishes, mostly along the Heilongjiang border. Harbin's government, believing a Soviet invasion to be imminent, set about building underground corridors, about three kilometres long, that were meant to house the whole of the city's population in the event of an attack. These were kept meticulously ready until 1985, when peace broke out.

Now they have a new use. The corridors have been turned into a thriving temple of free enterprise selling the latest fashions from Hong Kong. With the shelter the corridors offer from Harbin's −25°C cold, and with the hundreds of jobs this subterranean market has created, they must surely be Russia's greatest gift to the chilly city.

The old model was simple. Information was stored in the DNA of genes. When needed, it was transcribed into template molecules known as messenger RNAs. Then a piece of machinery called a ribosome translated the template, constructing a protein as it went.

Later the model got a bit more complicated. Genes, it was discovered, consist of lengths of informative DNA interspersed with apparently meaningless stretches known as introns. Before a messenger RNA template can be copied into proteins the introns must be removed from it—a process known as splicing.

Now things are getting more complicated still. In the past few years a new phenomenon has been discovered. Sometimes, after the template has been made and the introns removed, the RNA is edited. Sometimes, indeed, it is edited heavily. In the most extreme examples known so far, more than half of the information needed to make a protein has not come from the original gene. Instead, it has been edited into the messenger RNA template.

ANNOUNCE AN EXAMPLE

Some paragraphs illustrate a previous point, opening with *Take* or *Consider* or having a *for example* near the front.

Attacking corporate fat cats has plenty of voter appeal, particularly when few people have yet to feel much benefit from

Britain's economic recovery. But there is no reason to suppose that the bulk of Labour politicians are only pretending to hold these views. And, on their merits, none of these attacks on profitable firms is sustainable.

The IPPR study, *for instance,* criticises the external costs and regional concentrations of supermarket chains using criteria so unreasonable that they would condemn most large industries. The Office of Fair Trading and the Monopolies and Mergers Commission studied supermarkets several times but found no proof of serious market failure or lack of competition.

Once upon a time New York's bankers drank lunch-time martinis; blue-collar Texans drank beer as they cruised the highway; and sophisticates everywhere could tell the difference between bourbon and rye. So much for lost hedonism. Alcohol consumption in America has been declining for the past 17 years, and today no figure with a claim to respectability — politician, businessman or banker — can risk even a single drink at lunch-time. Alcohol is a poison or a distraction; and its use is to be shunned, or indeed restricted.

Last week, *for example,* President Clinton stood beside Brenda Frazier, whose daughter Ashley had been killed by a drunk driver, and announced plans, to apply first on federal property and then across the whole country, to lower the alcohol level at which a driver can still legally drive. "There is hardly a family or community in America", said the president, "that hasn't been touched by drunk driving."

STRING EXAMPLES TOGETHER

You can also string examples together across paragraphs — either to extend them or to contrast them.

Sometimes it irks allies such as the French to see America grab so much of the credit for its mediating efforts. But as even the French admit, America is in a league of its own in this business. No other country can match its clout and its credibility with parties on all sides of an argument. Bosnia is the most striking example: a catastrophe so long as America kept its distance, on the mend once America started to lead.

There are other, less conspicuous examples. Last January an almost comic fracas over a tiny rock in the Aegean briefly threatened to escalate into an alarming conflict between two NATO members, Greece and Turkey. While the European powers looked the other way, and the United Nations called for restraint, the Greeks and the Turks turned to America to help sort the matter out—which, after multiple telephone calls to agitated leaders in Athens and Ankara, it duly did. The next day one of the America diplomats involved, Richard Holbrooke, the star of the Dayton peace talks on Bosnia, described the incident as a microcosm of modern American foreign policy.

But cuts here are political dynamite. Take the government's planned cuts in state help to unemployed and poor people with mortgages, on which spending has grown from £31 in 1979 to £1.1 billion today. Tony Blair, Labour's leader, is determined to stop the cuts. So is Nicholas Winterton, a Tory right-winger keen on cuts in general, who threatens to lead a rebellion against Mr Lilley's plans.

Or take the recent cuts in non-means-tested invalidity benefits. Many of those claiming the benefits are middle-income people who had to retire early and were advised by their employers to top up their pensions with the benefit. And what are many doing with their new-found leisure? Spending it at Tory coffee mornings, that's what. Mr Lilley has warned colleagues that opposition to cuts in invalidity payments has yet to peak.

UNDERMINE

By undermining the point of the first paragraph, you can propel your argument in the next. You can either be subtle:

For the first time since 1985, the Geneva-based World Economic Forum has rated the U.S. economy the most competitive in the world. The U.S. Council on Competitiveness, a private coalition of leaders from industry, labor and education, recently concluded that "the United States has significantly strengthened its competitive position in critical technologies during the past five years."

But just like word of Mark Twain's death, *reports of America's industrial revival are exaggerated.* The Sonys, Respironics, and Medrads are isolated islands of success in a sea of economic stagnation. They are what Richard Florida, director of the Center for Economic Development at Carnegie-Mellon University in Pittsburgh, calls deceptive examples of "reindustrialization amidst deindustrialization, pockets of growth that co-exist with the continued decline of some sectors and firms."

or blatant:

Nippon Steel's Yawata works on the island of Kyushu might stand as a symbol of post-war Japan. In its heyday in the early

1970s, when the economy was still booming and costs were low, the Yawata works employed 46,000. Just 6,400 people work there today. The country's big blast-furnace steel makers have been elbowed aside by minimills, which are technologically more advanced, and by rivals from countries where costs are lower.

There is one catch with this tale: *it is not true.* Although employment has indeed fallen in Japan's five integrated steel makers, they are thriving. Against all expectations, Nippon Steel, Kawasaki Steel, Sumitomo Metal Industries, Kobe Steel and Nippon Kashuha have brought production costs to within a whisker of the world's most efficient producer, South Korea's Pohang Iron & Steel Company (POSCO). The five can now churn out hot-rolled coil at about $300 a tonne compared with POSCO's $270 a tonne.

In the example below, a question does the undermining:

The results are visible on the streets of Warsaw, Prague, and Budapest. Shops are full of western goods. Where grim-faced policemen once stared down pedestrians, street vendors now hawk their wares. The Communist Party's former headquarters in Warsaw houses Poland's infant stock exchange. Prague's Wenceslas Square is festooned with colourful advertisements. Hundreds of thousands of local entrepreneurs have started small businesses. Scores of western law firms, consultants and accountants are setting up offices. From all appearances, business is booming.

Or is it? By most measures, Eastern Europe is in the grip of a prolonged and savage recession. After declining by 8% or so last year, the five countries' GDPs are expected to drop another 8% this year. Industrial output has declined even faster, by 17% last year and probably 11% this year. Like all statistics about Eastern Europe, these figures are endlessly disputed and have to be taken with a large pinch of salt. They may paint too grim a picture because they underestimate the growth of private businesses. Yet these countries are clearly in economic trauma.

EXEMPLARY PARAGRAPHS

Xan Smiley

A GOLDEN AGE OF DISCOVERY

Artificial satellites can read car number plates. They can photograph pebbles on mountain-tops. They can gaze into hitherto unfathomed trenches bigger than the Grand Canyon in the bowels of the oceans. Loggers, mineral seekers and road-builders are rolling back tropical rain forest like a floor rug and destroying the lives of the world's last "noble savages." *Ice, mountain, sea, and desert no longer resist the wiles of modern man and his machines.*

The world has shrivelled in the past two centuries. It was only in 1806 that two American explorers, the unsuitably named Meriwether Lewis and his friend William Clark, became the first people (you can bet that no pre-Columbian personage would have been so mad) to trudge across the North American continent. A hundred years ago vast swathes of Africa were still unknown to outsiders. *It was only in 1909 and 1912 that* Homo supposedly sapiens managed to stand on the

[margin annotations: Series of descriptive details; Conclude with the point; Lead with the point; Parallel structure]

North and South Poles. Even into the second half of this century, chunks of the world, even people, were unknown to inquisitive industrial man. After the second world war, unheard of peoples—one of them 60,000 strong—living in the highlands and valleys of Papua New Guinea were "contacted" by outsiders for the first time. **Much terra was incognita.**

In the past few decades, the world's remotest places and peoples have been visited, classified, chartered, often desecrated. While vulnerable tribes have died out, backpackers can hitch a ride (not that easily, it is true) across the Sahara. Mount Everest, the world's highest peak, first scaled in 1953, has now been climbed at least 750 times—by 33 people, two years ago, on one day. Tourists have been flown to the North Pole. Eccentrics cross the Atlantic in—as a seriously record-breaking explorer, Sir Ranulph Fiennes, puts it—"ever tinier amphibious bottles of gin."

But hundreds, if not thousands, of peaks and mountain routes are *still* to be climbed. Numerous Arctic and Antarctic challenges are *still* to be met. The rain forests of the Amazon, parts of Africa, New Guinea (that huge island north of Australia made up of Irian Jaya, part of Indonesia, to the west, and Papua New Guinea to the east) all *still* bulge with mystery; *whole ranges of flora, fauna, and even groups of people are scantily known about within them.*

More than 70% of the earth's surface is water; and the oceans, on some measures, are the richest of all places in biodiversity—but

Point: much about the world is yet unknown

the least known. Only once has a person (or two people together, to be precise) plumbed the depths of the deepest ocean trench. On land and sea, 97% of the world's species have

Conclude with a comment

yet—by some recent calculations—to be "discovered." **Yes, 97%.**

*Exploration means many things. **One** is* finding places that have never felt the imprint of a human foot. **Another** is satisfying the yen of industrial man to seek out "new" isolated peoples, whose languages or way of life have barely been recorded or analyzed—

Binding: announce and number

Lead with the point; join details using conjunctions

let alone understood. A **third** thing usually thought of as belonging with exploration is the feat of human skill or will power among nature's elements, gauged not just by "first visits" to mountain tops or ocean bottoms, but by novel or ever tougher methods of getting there.

A **fourth** type of exploration is scientific. Earth science rather than anthropology or the personal challenges to a man's (and, increasingly a woman's) mind and body against the elements is nowadays perhaps the biggest exploratory motor. To explore—defined in the Oxford dictionary as "to examine (a country, etc.) by going through it" has become more of a "micro" business. These days, mere "going through" is not good enough. Exploration, to more and more people, means examination of whole ecosystems. *In this respect, most of the world is still up for exploratory grabs.*

Transition: continuation of announce and number

Conclude with the point

The vain, the curious, and the greedy
The old yardsticks still provide the vain, the

Lead with the point

philanthropic, the greedy, the religious, the curious, the intrepid and the simply crazy with thousands of challenges not yet met. **Forget,** for a moment, that perhaps 40m species of flora and fauna have yet to be classified. **Think** of the places and even peoples that have never been "discovered," the human feats of travel waiting to be achieved.

Most of the world's extremities and most extremely remote places have been visited—but by no means all. **Deserts have been** pretty thoroughly tramped across—though it is surprising how many "firsts," even by car, are not yet in record books. Most of the world's **forests have been,** roughly speaking, visited and mapped. But many have not been scrutinized. At the simplest level, numerous ***jungle patches have probably never been*** trodden by industrial man before. In Africa, places such as the Ndoki forest, on the border of Congo and Cameroon, or the dense strip of jungle between the Laulaba river (as the upper reaches of the Zaire river, once the Congo, are known) and one of the tributaries, the Lomami, are still virtually unexplored by outsiders. And challenges of survival and travel, especially if you eschew machinery, exist even in well-trodden Africa. It was only in 1986, for instance, that someone (a duo, actually—a similar solo trip has yet to be done) went from west to east by camel across the continent, bisecting the Sahara.

The forests of Borneo, Sarawak and New Guinea, though well traversed in the past two decades, contain pockets of sketchily charted

Parallel structure: direct address

Lead with the point (point elaborating on point of previous paragraph—building momentum); list disparate details

Parallel structure: one verb form

Conclude with the point

territory. *Indeed, all the great jungles of Asia, Africa, and South America, though photographed from the sky, are full of unsolved mystery.*

Point implied in a series of details

The satellite camera cannot peer under the rain forest's canopy, which guards the richest repositories of unknown plant and animal life on land. Only recently have scientists begun to use special cranes and inflatable rafts to snoop into and under the tapestry of the forest roof. Yet the Amazonian ecology is so diverse that some patches, even of an isolated acre or two, may contain species of plants, for instance, that grow nowhere else on the planet. And even when they glimpse the jungle from the sky, the satellites—and their human interpreters—are fallible. Some seemingly authoritative recent atlases, according to John Hemming, director of the Royal Geographical Society, still make "gross errors" in delineating rivers in Amazonia.

Lead with the point; list disparate details

Much is not yet known about the earth's cold bits. As it is landless (though not iceless) for hundreds of miles around the North Pole, the Arctic is also more of a place for the old-fashioned beat-the-elements explorer. Only in 1968 did Wally Herbert, an Englishman, manage the first surface crossing of the Arctic Ocean, from land to land, by way of the North Pole. Nobody, alone, has ever traversed the whole Arctic Ocean, nor gone from one side of the Antarctic continent to the other single-handed, "unsupported" and without mechanical vehicles. Even the rim of Greenland, that large Danish-owned island, has never been circum-navigated—and when a British mountaineer, Chris Bonington, and a fellow explorer, Sir Robin Knox-Johnson, climbed what they thought was the tallest mountain in Greenland in 1991, it turned out that the map-makers had marked the wrong summit. Other exploratory inadequacies are equally revealing: the world's northernmost island, off Greenland was not discovered until 1978.

Lead with the point; list disparate details

The Antarctic is sometimes called the "last major unexplored region of the world." Half as big again as the United States, it is valued both for the challenge it still offers to the intrepid and for its trove of undisclosed knowledge sought by the scientist. After the tragi-heroic competition of 1911–12, when a Norwegian, Roald Amundsen, and his team with dogs beat Robert Scott and his five-man team from Britain (all of whom perished) to become the first men at the South Pole, numerous challenges remained to be met. Not until 1993 did a Norwegian, Erling Kagge, become the first person to reach the South Pole, solo, by land and "unsupported."

Continuation of previous point

And whole ranges of Antarctic mountains have never been climbed. Mr. Bonington is heading for one of them soon. One free-standing pinnacle, about 1,000 metres (3,300 feet high) is probably the tallest such tower in the world—unclimbed, of course. **"Very, very exciting,"** he says.

Conclude with a comment

Lead with the point

List example

*But scientists are equally **excited** by Antarctica's potential for clues to understanding, among other things, the world's climate.* **To *that end,*** scientists at the European

Transition: repeat word from previous paragraph

Project for Ice Coring in Antarctica (EPICA) are embarking on a five-year scheme based at a research station 1,000km (625 miles) from its nearest neighbor, where the average temperature is −45°C. The ice-crust they will investigate is about 3km thick.

A most dangerous sport

Lead with the point; list disparate details

Though seemingly less remote, because more relentlessly explored over many more years, mountains are a source of extraordinary attraction for explorers. Here, too there is a good generation or so to go before anybody can say "everything has been done." Mountaineering is a bizarre activity because it combines so many contradictory feature of humanity: individualism and teamwork, a thirst for survival inspired by a thirst for danger, speed and muscle matched by canniness and steadiness, the practical rubbing against the poetic.

Lead with the point

Two ways to tackle a mountain have been called "the anarchists" and "the organizers." Mountaineers, it hardly needs saying, plan in detail and with ever fancier tackle, how to thwart the elements. Yet many of the hardier ones, rightly in their terms, complain the modern practice is making such heights as Everest too easy. "Doing more with less," is the phrase that mountaineers such as Mr. Bonington like to use. "Easy" here means "not quite so terrifyingly hard." No sport continues to lead so many of the top practitioners to their deaths. "Simple" Everest has killed at least 120 people in the past four decades.

Not until 1978 did Reinhold Messner, an Austrian who many think is the world's finest living mountaineer, climb Everest in a colleague's company without bottled oxygen. All in all, the most difficult mountain to climb is the world's second tallest, K2, at the western end of the Himalayan range. In 1986, 13 people were killed trying to get up (or down) it. Alison Hargreaves, a Briton who was the first woman up Everest on "normal" air, died on K2 last summer.

But any of the 14 Himalayan peaks which rise to more than 8,000 metres still offer fearsome challenges; once you have gone up the most straightforward way, new "lines," as mountaineers call their routes, are still to be sought out—though not too many are left. Only two climbers—Mr. Messner was the first—have scaled all 14. The other, a Pole, has since been killed. "Any of those mountains," says Stephen Venables, the first Briton up Everest without extra oxygen, "involves difficult climbing—your mind and body are teetering on the edge of control." And some terrifying unclimbed routes beckon: the west face of K2, the east face of Kanchenjunga, the west face of Makalu (probably the stiffest challenge of the lot), several oxygenless ascents and a number of peak-to-peak ridge traverses.

Of the 400 or so peaks between 7,000 and 8,000 metres, more than 100 remain unclimbed. With dollar-desirous China opening its mountains to outsiders, vast new ranges are offering fresh challenges: southeast Tibet, for instance, has a range as long as the Alps (and much taller) where outside professionals have hardly trodden. And the Himalaya is by no means the only range to lure the would-be record-breaker. Some of the Tepui mountains, sheer slabs of unscaled sandstone rising out of the wilderness of southern Venezuela, are magnificently inaccessible.

Lead with the point; list disparate details

***Another** sort that now offers one of the biggest array of possible "firsts" is speleology, better known as caving.* One of the world's top cavers, Andrew Eavis, a Briton, reckons that even in Britain, two-thirds of the country's caves have never been penetrated—and across the sea in Ireland, the proportion, he thinks, is 90%. Especially where there is limestone, caves lure the daring and the curious. Aerial photography plus greater geological savvy can predict where they are likely to be. China and New Guinea are prime candidates for a burst of cavernous exploration.

Transition: count

Point implied in a series of details

In the densest tropical rain forest of the remote Gunung Mulu National Park in Sarawak (part of Malaysia), **Mr. Eavis** and colleagues found what is the largest known cave in he world: 400 metres long and in places 250 metres high **The Hollywood Bowl could fit inside.** Often the cavers' challenge is to dig to enter: sometimes you must swim underwater through riverine entrances. **Mr. Eavis's** world-beating Sarawak Chamber requires a kilometre-long swim and a waterfall ascent—all in helmet-borne torchlight—before you can reach it. **"We are relatively normal people,"** he says of his fellow speleo-fans.

Comment is conversational

Binding: repetition

Conclude with a comment

The vasty deep

As for the relatively unexplored sea, nobody till recently was able to get far down. Man without mechanical artifice can dip only about ten metres before destroying himself. Even with a "self-contained underwater breathing apparatus" (SCUBA), invented in the 1940s, going 50 metres deep pushes an expert's luck. *Yet the seas are deeper than the mountains are high.* The Mariana trench in mid-Pacific is more than 11,000 metres deep. (Everest, by contrast, is 8,848 metres high). Only two men have ever been there, a French man, Jacques Piccard, and an American, Don Walsh, in the Trieste bathyscope in 1960. Nobody but a Japanese team has been so deep again. **Most scientists say they are not missing much. Only 3% of the ocean is under the 6,000 metre mark.**

All the same, the ocean's average depth is 3,700 metres. And recent discoveries, often by means of remotely operated vehicles (ROVs) and autonomous underwater vehicles (AUVs) show that far more life exists in the deep than most people had guessed. In fact, the oceans almost certainly contain the greatest biodiversity on the planet's surface, whether water-covered or not. New types of bacteria and viruses, as well as an array of new plant and fish life, exist in fantastic abundance: newly discovered sea-worms, mussels, even a huge 20-metre-long squid. Amazingly high temperatures, of more than 400°C have been measured thousands of metres down. Hydrothermal vents are blowing away more than 2,000 metres below sea-level. Sink an-

Undermine in the middle to make the point

Conclude with a comment

Lead with the point; list disparate details

Transition: undermine previous paragraph

other 1,300 metres, and the Pacific Ocean is carpeted with an array of manganese, cobalt and countless other mineral valuables. Little volcanoes like wobbly black factory chimneys, known as "black smokers," are down there belching out metal sulphides and chemicals.

Most scientists think it not hugely useful for people to be squinting in person at minerals or fish: robots' photographs will do. *But for those seeking new minerals, working out how continents were formed (by plate-tectonics) or predicting climatic and atmospheric change, the ability to explore the depths of the ocean opens a staggering new scientific vista.*

On dry land, exploring for new flora, fauna, and even human life remains as exciting as ever—guess as you might that few or no unknown big animals, let alone peoples, are left. *But you would be wrong there, too.* In Vietnam a completely new species of large mammal, the vu kwang ox (which looks a bit like an oryx), has recently been identified, so has a kind of giant muntjak (something like a fallow deer), and recent whispers from Sumatra suggest a new type of primate may have been found. A leading British ethno-biologist thinks a mega-therium, a sort of giant ground sloth which may stand as high as a giraffe, and was thought to have become extinct several millennia ago, may lurk in the vastnesses of the Amazon basin.

Though less likely, discovering "new people" is also possible. "First contact" yarns ped-

---

Side notes:

Undermine at the end to make a point

Undermine immediately to make a point

Lead with the point; list examples

dled by fame-seekers have to be listened to warily. "New" peoples are often splinters from "old" ones. But in 1995, both in Irian Jaya and in the Brazilian forest, people previously uncontacted by outsiders may have been found. Over a period of two decades both in the Amazon basin (where 370 or so indigenous groups exist) and in New Guinea (where there are more than a thousand), people unknown to the outside world, some of whose languages were sometimes undeciphered even by their neighbors, have come to light. Study of many well-known peoples living in broadly pre-industrial ways has been so patchy that social anthropologists have eons of research to do—besides which, the people they study never stop evolving into "different" people.

Even in Africa linguists occasionally discover languages never before identified. Defining a language is tricky. Many cover a seamless continuum. But of the 6,528 or so living languages listed by the Summer Institute of Linguistics in Britain, hundreds are not fully understood outside the group that speaks them. *Even in* Nigeria (with 420 languages indexed, out of Africa's 1,995) a tiny new one popped up two years ago. *More worrying, for those who would resist global homogeneity, is languages' galloping disappearance: some linguists reckon that more than 95% may vanish within a century, leaving a shrinking core of some 300 living tongues.* **Many need to be caught on tape before they fly into oblivion.**

Margin notes:
- Repeat a structure
- Undermine at the end to make a point
- Conclude with a comment

Discovering yourself

Point implied in a series of details

"The possibilities for exploration and discovery are infinite," says Mr. Hemming. "New species are evolving faster than man can extinguish old ones." Explorers, he believes, are entering "a new golden age of discovery." Although he has experienced hardship and danger (a close friend was killed by Amazonian Indians) during decades of exploration, Mr. Hemming stresses the scientific and philanthropic side—and has fought hard to defend the rights, indeed the survival, of indigenous peoples threatened by modern man.

Lead with the point; list disparate details

Science may now predominate in exploration, but romance, poetry, heroism still call. Even boffins and flea taxonomists may sometimes admit that exploration is also about peering into their souls and asking who they are. Mountaineers, in particular, are unabashed about their urge to compete, both against the horrifying hunks of rock they clamber and often die on, and against their fellow men. Mountaineering, says Mr.

Conclude with comments

Bonington, should not be made "safe, tame, and boring. Man should not overimpose himself on the mountain." Mr. Venables talks of the need to "give the mountain a chance."

Continuation of previous point

Sir Wilfred Thesiger, 85, last of the old school of British explorers, admits even to competing against the indigenous people with whom he lived in the deserts. Among the Rashid of southern Arabia, he candidly admits: "I had to meet the challenge of the desert on equal terms with them. I could

Transition: continuing list of quotations from previous paragraph

equal them physically, the real challenge was to live up to them mentally and morally. But they were the only people I couldn't compete with on a moral level—in honesty, generosity, loyalty, courage. They always thought they were superior to everyone else—and they were."

SOURCES

AN APPROACH TO PARAGRAPHS

Getting off to a good start

Still an Unequal World, Human Development Report (Washington, D.C.: United Nations Development Programme, 1995), p. 29.

"Clearing the Killing Fields," *The Economist* 347, no. 8066 (2 May 1998): 73.

"Word of Mouse," *The Economist* 347, no. 8066 (2 May 1998): 57.

W. John Moore, "An Albatross Named Bill," *National Journal* 26, no. 42 (15 October 1994): 2406.

Solange De Santis, "Nice Bagpipes, Man, But Don't You Feel a Draft in That Skirt?" *Wall Street Journal,* 12 October 1994, sec. A, p. 1.

Paul Krugman, "Not for Ordinary Folk," (www.redherring.com/mag/school.html) issue 38.

"Triumphant abroad," in *Survey: Asia's Emerging Economies, The Economist* 321, no. 7733 (16 November 1991): 7.

Meg Greenfield, "Unsexing the Military," *Newsweek* 129, no. 24 (16 June 1997): 80.

E. M. Forster, *Aspects of the Novel* (New York: Harcourt, Brace, 1955), p. 83.

Summing up

A. Leon Higginbotham, Jr., "Breaking Thurgood Marshall's Promise," *New York Times Magazine,* 18 January 1998, sec. 6, p. 29.

Jonathan Broder, "Tangier," *Smithsonian* 29, no. 4 (July 1988): 100.

"The Last Communists," *The Economist* 346, no. 8051 (17 January 1998): 21.

"From Morgan's Nose to Milken's Wig," in *Survey: International Finance*, *The Economist* 319, no. 7704 (27 April 1991): 12.

"The Somali Spectre," *The Economist* 333, no. 7883 (1 October 1994): 20.

1. UNIFY YOUR PARAGRAPHS AROUND STRONG POINTS

Be clear about your subject

"Where the Old China Lives On," *The Economist* 334, no. 7897 (14 January 1995): 33.

"The Interminable Net," *The Economist* 338, no. 7951 (3 February 1996): 70.

Make a strong point

"Sacking the Powers-That-Be," *The Economist* 333, no. 7884 (8 October 1994): 99.

"No Going Back," *The Economist* 335, no. 7917 (3 June 1995): 17.

"China Odyssey," *The Economist* 337, no. 7937 (21 October 1995): 91.

Be sure every sentence bears on the point

"Nobel Game Theory," *Wall Street Journal*, 12 October 1994, sec. A, p. 14.

Stephen Kinzer, "A Climate for Demagogues," *Atlantic* 273, no. 2 (February 1994): 21–22.

"Risk and Reward," in *Survey: Asia's Emerging Economies*, *The Economist* 321, no. 7773 (16 November 1991): 6.

Repeat a key term

"The Death of Distance," *The Economist* 336, no. 7934 (30 September 1995): 6–7.

"Scribble, Scribble, Mr Gibbon," *The Economist* 334, no. 7897 (14 January 1995): 75.

David Shribman, "Mr. Speaker," *New York Times Book Review*, 21 April 1996, sec. 7, p. 15.

Repeat a sentence structure—for sentences doing the same work

David Shribman, "Mr. Speaker," *New York Times Book Review*, 21 April 1996, sec. 7, p. 15.

"If Wall Street Falters," *The Economist* 340, no. 7973 (6 July 1996): 19.

Herbert Stein, "High Life on the Potomac," *Slate* (www.slate.com) 17 April 1997.

Count the elements

Herbert Stein, "Reading the Inaugurals," *Slate* (www.slate.com), 10 January 1997.

"Still an Unequal World," The Human Development Report 1995 (New York: Oxford University Press, 1995), p. 29.

"Just Like Ringing a Bell," in *Survey: The Music Business. The Economist* 321, no. 7738 (21 December 1991): 4.

Signal what's to come

"Can Labour Learn to Love Profit?" *The Economist* 334, no. 7897 (14 January 1995): 49.

"The Voice of Economic Nationalism," *Atlantic* 282 no. 1 (July 1998): 100.

"The Shan Connection," *The Economist* 338, no. 7947 (6 January 1996): 27.

Stick to one subject

"Endicott Peabody," *The Economist* 345, no. 8047 (13 December 1997): 80.

"How to Kill Your Multimedia Industry," *The Economist* 333, no. 7889 (12 November 1994): 87.

"It Seems to Me," *Slate* (www.slate.com), 6 February 1997.

Stick to one verb form

"Paradise Retained," *The Economist* 338, no. 7951 (3 February 1996): 72.

Henry R. Luce, *The American Century* (New York: Farrar and Rinehart, 1941), p. 32.

2. MAKE YOUR POINTS IN COMPELLING WAYS

Lead with the point and support it

"Unjammed," *The Economist* 347, no. 8069 (23 May 1998): 74.

Ken Wells, "The Ancient Baobab Is a Sight to Behold, and That's the Rub," *Wall Street Journal*, 20 March 1997, sec. A, p. 1.

"For Richer, for Poorer," *The Economist* 333, no. 7888 (5 November 1994): 20.

Lead with the point and conclude with a comment

"Geo-political Earthquake," *The Economist* 335, no. 7917 (3 June 1995): 45.

Thomas T. Samaras, "Let's Get Small," *Harper's* 289, no. 1736 (January 1995): 32–33.

"Banking on the Fed," *The Economist* 337, no. 7937 (21 October 1995): 80.

"The Fundamentals of Editing," *The Economist* 338, no. 7957 (16 March 1996): 82.

"At Last, a People's Art," *The Economist* 346, no. 8051 (17 January 1998): 77.

Lead with the point and, using conjunctions, join details

"The Trouble with Teams," *The Economist* 334, no. 7897 (14 January 1995): 61.

"Blood Disorder," *The Economist* 338, no. 7958 (23 March 1996): 49.

Lead with the point and list disparate details

Jeffrey Goldberg, "Our Africa," *New York Times Magazine*, 2 March 1997, sec. 6, p. 76.

"One Swallow," *The Economist* 342, no. 8009 (22 March 1997): 65.

Lead with the point and follow it with a bulleted list

UNDP–World Bank, *Water and Sanitation Program Annual Report*, July 1994–June 1995 (Washington, D.C.: World Bank, 1996), pp. 64–65.

UNDP, *Human Development Report 1995* (New York: Oxford University Press, 1995), p. 39.

Conclude with the point after introducing the subject

"Slicing the Cake," *The Economist* 333, no. 7888 (5 November 1994): 13.

Paul Krugman, "The CPI and the Rat Race," *Slate* (www.slate.com), 21 December 1996.

Conclude with the point after listing disparate details

"To Bury or to Praise," *The Economist* 337, no. 7937 (21 October 1995): 23.

"The Mall of Dreams," *The Economist* 339, no. 7964 (4 May 1996): 23.

Make the point in the middle

"The Aspic of History," *The Economist* 338, no. 7947 (6 January 1996): 67.
Richard Rorty, "Demonizing the Academy," *Harper's* 289, no. 1736 (January 1995): 13.

Undermine a premise at the end of a paragraph

"The Age of Social Transformation," *Atlantic* 274, no. 5 (November 1994): 64.
"Owners vs. Managers," *The Economist* 333, no. 7884 (8 October 1994): 20.

Undermine a premise immediately

Russell Jacoby, "The Ivory Tower Obscurity Fetish," *Harper's,* 289, no. 1732 (September 1994): 26.
Herbert Stein, "The Cubist Republican," *Slate* (www.slate.com), 15 May 1997.

Undermine a premise in the middle of the paragraph

"The Age of Social Transformation," *Atlantic* 274, no. 5 (November 1994): 59.
"Under New Management," *The Economist* 333, no. 7884 (8 October 1994): 21.

Start with a question and answer it immediately

"Short Guys Finish Last," *The Economist* 337, no. 7946 (23 December 1995): 19.
"The Survival of the Fittest," *The Economist* 337, no. 7937 (21 October 1995): 92.
"Doubts, Hesitancy, Determination," *The Economist* 346, no. 8055 (14 February 1998): 51.
"A Sobering View," *The Economist* 334, no. 7897 (14 January 1995): 74.

Start with a question and answer it in succeeding sentences

"The Poor Get Richer," *The Economist* 333, no. 7888 (5 November 1994): 39.
Marcy Lamm, "A New York Court May Decide When a Cough Drop Gets Stale," *Wall Street Journal,* 18 June 1996, sec. B, p. 1.

Start with a question and answer it at the end

"The Philosopher's Pupil," *The Economist* 338, no. 7948 (13 January 1996): 77.

"On the Rocks," in *East Asian Economies Survey, The Economist* 346, no. 8058 (7 March 1998): 7.

Ask several questions and answer each immediately

"To Bury or to Praise," *The Economist* 337, no. 7937 (21 October 1995): 27.

Paul Krugman, "In Praise of Cheap Labor," *Slate* (www.slate.com), 20 March 1997.

Imply the point in a series of details or examples

"The Ups and Downs of Two Italian Rivals," *The Economist* 342, no. 8008 (15 March 1997): 56.

Andrew Jacobs, "Where Prices Are out of This World," *New York Times*, 18 November 1997, sec. A, p. 16.

Imply the point in a series of questions

Norman Myers, *Ultimate Security: The Environmental Basis of Political Stability* (Washington D.C.: Island Press, 1993), p. 153.

"To Bury or to Praise," *The Economist* 337, no. 7937 (21 October 1995): 23.

"A Disease of Society," *The Economist* 333, no. 7888 (5 November 1994): 48.

Imply the point by presenting two sides

"How to Sit on a Useless Pile," *The Economist* 335, no. 7917 (3 June 1995): 33.

Bruce Stokes, "Out of the Rubble," *National Journal* 26, no. 42 (15 October 1994): 2398.

Imply the point in an analogy or syllogism

"From Morgan's Nose to Milken's Wig," in *Survey: International Finance, The Economist* 319, no. 7704 (27 April 1991): 12.

"Your Obedient Servant," in *Survey: International Finance, The Economist* 319, no. 7704 (27 April 1991): 43.

Deirdre N. McCloskey, *The Rhetoric of Economics* (Madison: University of Wisconsin Press, 1985), p. 3.

3. LINK YOUR PARAGRAPHS

Repeat a word or phrase from the end of the preceding paragraph

"O Rare John Smith," *The Economist* 335, no. 7917 (3 June 1995): 32.
"The Fundamentals of Editing," *The Economist* 338, no. 7957 (16 March
    1996): 81.

Turn the repeated word into a question

"Who Speaks for Cyberspace?" *The Economist* 334, no. 7897 (14 January
    1995): 64.
"Sad Dreams by the Nile," *The Economist* 335, no. 7917 (3 June 1995): 35.

Repeat an opening word or phrase

"Model Behaviour," *The Economist* 346, no. 8057 (28 February 1998): 80.
"The Aspic of History," *The Economist* 338, no. 7947 (6 January 1996): 67.

Signal what's to come

Julie Kosterlitz, "The Second Wave," *National Journal* 26, no. 42 (15
    October 1994): 2393.
"Fazed," *The Economist* 335, no. 7917 (3 June 1995): 69.

Establish pairs across paragraphs

Edward Luttwak, "The CIA Is Déclassé," *Slate* (www.slate.com), 29 March
    1997.

*Ask a question at the end of one paragraph and answer it at the beginning
of the next*

"A Blue Chip on a New Block," *The Economist* 334, no. 7897 (14 January
    1995): 65.
"Italy's Millennial Tangle," *The Economist* 345, no. 8047 (13 December
    1997): 46.

Ask a question at the beginning of the second paragraph

"Gold: A Repulsive Metal but a Noble One," *The Economist* 335, no. 7917
    (3 June 1995): 76.
"Consciences and Consequences," *The Economist* 335, no. 7917 (3 June
    1995): 13.

"Germany's 'Silverbullet,' " *The Economist* 346, no. 8051 (17 January 1998): 69.

Make a comment

"Mediterranean Blues," *The Economist* 334, no. 7897 (14 January 1995): 14.

"The Many-Handed Mr. Eizenstat," *The Economist* 346, no. 8052 (24 January 1998): 30.

Count

"Valuing Virtue," *The Economist* 347, no. 8070 (30 May 1998): 57.

"Scribble, scribble Mr. Gibbon," *The Economist* 334, no. 7897 (14 January 1995): 75.

Place paragraphs in time

"The Russians Are Coming," *The Economist* 334, no. 7897 (14 January 1995): 34.

"The Fundamentals of Editing," *The Economist* 338, no. 7957 (16 March 1996): 81.

Announce an example

"Can Labour Learn to Love Profit?" *The Economist* 334, no. 7897 (14 January 1995): 49.

"Let the Law, at Least, Be Clearheaded," *The Economist* 346, no. 8059 (14 March 1998): 25.

String examples together

"Leadership on the Cheap," *The Economist* 339, no. 7964 (4 May 1996): 30.

"Principles of Surgery," *The Economist* 334, no. 7897 (14 January 1995): 52.

Undermine

Bruce Stokes, "Out of the Rubble," *National Journal* 26, no. 42 (15 October 1994): 2398.

"On a Roll," *The Economist* 345, no. 8038 (11 October 1997): 74.

"Jam Tomorrow," in *Survey: Business in Eastern Europe, The Economist* 320, no. 7725 (21 September 1991): 4.

EXEMPLARY PARAGRAPHS

"A Golden Age of Discovery," *The Economist* 337, no. 7946 (23 December 1995): 56–58.